HOGAN'S GOAT

✤

by William Alfred

AGAMEMNON

HOGAN'S GOAT

FARRAR, STRAUS & GIROUX

New York

HOGAN'S
♣ GOAT ♣

William Alfred

A. M. D. G.

for

John and Máire Sweeney

with love

Almost all of the place names in this play really exist; but none of these characters has ever lived except in my own mind. Any resemblance to any person living or dead is purely coincidental.

Persons in the Play

✣

MATTHEW STANTON, *leader of the Sixth Ward of Brooklyn*
KATHLEEN STANTON, *his wife*
EDWARD QUINN, *Mayor of Brooklyn*
FATHER STANISLAUS COYNE, *Pastor of St. Mary Star of the Sea*
JAMES "PALSY" MURPHY, *Boss of the city of Brooklyn*
JOHN "BLACK JACK" HAGGERTY, *Assistant Ward Leader*
MARIA HAGGERTY, *his wife, the Stantons' janitor*
JOSEPHINE FINN, *Maria Haggerty's niece*
PETEY BOYLE, *a hanger-on of Stanton's*
BESSIE LEGG, *a back-room girl*
ANN MULCAHY, *Father Coyne's housekeeper*
BOYLAN, *a policeman*
BILL, *a hanger-on of Quinn's*

A priest, a deckhand, a doctor, various constituents

HOGAN'S GOAT

♣

♣ 1 ♣

♣

Ten o'clock, the evening of Thursday, April 28, 1890. The parlor of Matthew Stanton's flat on the second floor of his house on Fifth Place, Brooklyn. The set is on two levels, the lower level containing the kitchen of the Haggertys, which is blacked out. To stage right there is a steep, narrow staircase. Enter MATTHEW STANTON, carrying a bottle of champagne. He is a handsome, auburn-haired man in his late thirties, dressed carefully in a four-buttoned suit of good serge, and a soft black hat. He bounds up the stairs and into his flat, and throws his hat on a chair and hides the bottle of champagne behind the sofa. The furnishings of the room are in period: the chairs are tufted and fringed, the mantelpiece covered with a lambrequin, the window heavily draped.

STANTON

Katie? Katie! Where the devil are you?
Come on out in the parlor.

> [*Enter* KATHLEEN STANTON, *closing the door behind her. She is tall and slim and dressed in a black broadcloth suit which brings out the redness of her hair and the whiteness of her skin*]

KATHLEEN

I wish you wouldn't take those stairs so fast;
They're wicked: you could catch your foot and fall—
I had a bit of headache and lay down.
Why, Mattie darling, what's the matter with you?
You're gray as wasps' nests.

STANTON

                    I'm to be the mayor!
No more that plug who runs the Court Café
And owes his ear to every deadbeat sport
With a favor in mind and ten cents for a ball,
But mayor of Brooklyn, and you the mayor's lady.
They caught Ned Quinn with his red fist in the till,
The Party of Reform, I mean, and we
"Are going to beat their game with restitution
And self-reform." Say something, can't you, Kate!

> [KATHLEEN *sits down heavily, and puts her hand
> to her temple*]

KATHLEEN

Oh, Mattie, Mattie.

STANTON

                    Jesus! Are you crying?
I've what I wanted since I landed here
Twelve years ago, and she breaks into tears.

KATHLEEN

It's that I'm—

STANTON

What? You're what?

KATHLEEN

Afraid.

STANTON

Kathleen,
Now please don't let's go into that again.

KATHLEEN
Would you have me tell you lies?

STANTON

I'd have you brave.

[KATHLEEN *rises angrily, and strides towards the
bedroom*]

Where are you going, Kate? To have a sulk?
Wait now, I'll fix a sugar teat for you,
Unless, of course, you'd rather suck your thumb,
Brooding in your room—

KATHLEEN

I have the name!
As well to have the game!

STANTON

It's riddles, is it?

HOGAN'S GOAT

KATHLEEN

Riddles be damned! You think me idiotic;
I might as well fulfill your good opinion—

[STANTON *walks towards her*]

Come near me, and I'll smash your face for you.

[STANTON *embraces her*]

STANTON

You're terrible fierce, you are. I wet me pants.

KATHLEEN

You clown, you'll spring my hairpins. Mattie, stop.

STANTON

Are these the hands are going to smash my face?
They're weak as white silk fans . . . I'm sorry, Kate:
You made me mad. And you know why?

KATHLEEN

                                 I do.
You're as afraid as I.

STANTON

                I am. I am.
You know me like the lashes of your eye—

KATHLEEN

That's more than you know me, for if you did,
You'd see what these three years have done to me—

[STANTON *breaks away from her*]

Now it's my turn to ask you where you're going.

STANTON

I begged you not to bring that up again.
What can I do?

KATHLEEN

You can tell Father Coyne,
And ask him to apply for dispensation,
And we can be remarried secretly.

STANTON

Now?

KATHLEEN

Yes, Matt, now. Before it is too late.
We aren't married.

STANTON

What was that in London,
The drunkard's pledge I took?

KATHLEEN

We're Catholics, Matt.
Since when can Catholics make a valid marriage
In a city hall? You have to tell the priest—

STANTON

Shall I tell him now? Do you take me for a fool
To throw away the mayor's chair for that?

HOGAN'S GOAT

[7]

KATHLEEN

I slink to Sunday Mass like a pavement nymph.
It's three years now since I made my Easter Duty,
Three years of telling Father Coyne that we
Receive at Easter Mass in the Cathedral,
Mortal Sin on Mortal Sin, Matt. If I died,
I'd go to Hell—

STANTON

                    I think the woman's crazy!

KATHLEEN

Don't you believe in God?

STANTON

                    Of course, I do.
And more, my dear, than you who think that He
Would crush you as a man would crush a fly
Because of some mere technical mistake—

KATHLEEN

Mere technical mistake? It's that now, is it?
A blasphemous marriage, three years' fornication,
And now presumption— Technical mistake!

[KATHLEEN *takes a cigarette out of a box on the*
table and lights it]

STANTON

I wish you wouldn't smoke them cigarettes.
High-toned though it may be in France and England,
It's a whore's habit here.

[*Pause*]

KATHLEEN

"Those cigarettes."
Don't try to hurt me, Matt. You know you can,
As I know I can you.

STANTON

What do you want!

KATHLEEN

I want to be your wife without disgrace.
I want my honor back. I want to live
Without the need to lie. I want you to keep faith.

STANTON

Not now! Not now!

KATHLEEN

You've said that for three years.
What is it you're afraid of?

STANTON

Losing out.
You do not know these people as I do.
They turn upon the ones they make most of.
They would on me, if given half a chance.
And if it got around that we were married
In an English City Hall, lose out we would.

KATHLEEN

Matt, losing out? What profit for a man
To gain the world, and lose his soul?

HOGAN'S GOAT

[9]

His soul!
That's Sunday school! That's convent folderol,
Like making half-grown girls bathe in their drawers
To put the shame of their own beauty in them,
And break their lives to bear the Church's bit.
We are not priests and nuns, but men and women.
The world religious give up is our world,
The only world we have. We have to win it
To do the bit of good we all must do;
And how are we to win the world unless
We keep the tricky rules its games are run by?
Our faith is no mere monastery faith.
It runs as fast as feeling to embrace
Whatever good it sees. And if the good
Is overgrown with bad, it still believes
God sets no traps, the bad will be cut down,
And the good push through its flowering to fruit.
Forget your convent school. Remember, Katie,
What the old women in the drowned boreens
Would say when cloudbursts beat their fields to slime,
And the potatoes blackened on their stalks
Like flesh gone proud. "Bad times is right," they'd say,
"But God is good: apples will grow again."
What sin have we committed? Marriage, Kate?
Is that a sin?

KATHLEEN
It is with us.

HOGAN'S GOAT

STANTON

                    Because
You feel it so. It isn't. It's but prudence.
What if they should make a scandal of us?

KATHLEEN

Could we be worse off than we are?

STANTON

                              Kathleen!

KATHLEEN

Could we be worse off than we are, I said?

STANTON

Could we! We could. You don't know poverty.
You don't know what it is to do without,
Not fine clothes only, or a handsome house,
But men's respect. I do. I have been poor.
"Mattie, will you run down to the corner,
And buy me some cigars" or "Mattie, get
This gentleman a cab." Nine years, I served
Ned Quinn and Agnes Hogan, day by day,
Buying my freedom like a Roman slave.
Will you ask me to put liberty at stake
To ease your scrupulous conscience? If you do,
You're not the woman that I took you for
When I married you. Have you no courage, Kate?

KATHLEEN

Will you lecture me on courage? Do you dare?
When every time I walk those stairs to the street
I walk to what I know is an enemy camp.
I was not raised like you. And no offense,
Please, Mattie, no offense. I miss my home.
Whore's habit it may be to smoke, as you say,
But it brings back the talk we used to have
About old friends, new books, the Lord knows what,
On our first floor in Baggot Street in Dublin.
This following you think so much about,
We live in Mortal Sin for fear you'll lose it,
I never knew the likes of them to talk to,
Person to person. They were cooks and maids,
Or peasants at the country houses, Matt.
All they can find to talk of, servants' talk,
Serfs' talk, eternal tearing down.
I'm like a woman banished and cut off.
I've you and May in the flat downstairs. That's all.
Don't tell me I don't know what poverty is.
What bankruptcy is worse than loneliness.
They say the sense of exile is the worst
Of all the pains that torture poor damned souls.
It is that sense I live with every day.

STANTON

Are you the only exile of us all?
You slept your crossing through in a rosewood berth
With the swells a hundred feet below your portholes,
And ate off china on a linen cloth,

With the air around you fresh as the first of May.
I slept six deep in a bunk short as a coffin
Between a poisoned pup of a seasick boy
And a slaughtered pig of a snorer from Kildare,
Who wrestled elephants the wild nights through,
And sweated sour milk. I wolfed my meals,
Green water, and salt beef, and wooden biscuits,
On my hunkers like an ape, in a four-foot aisle
As choked as the one door of a burning school.
I crossed in mid-December: seven weeks
Of driving rain that kept the hatches battened
In a hold so low of beam a man my height
Could never lift his head. And I couldn't wash.
Water was low; the place was like an icehouse;
And girls were thick as field mice in a haystack
In the bunk across. I would have died of shame,
When I stood in the landing shed of this "promised land,"
As naked as the day I first saw light,
Defiled with my own waste like a dying cat,
And a lousy red beard on me like a tinker's,
While a bitch of a doctor, with his nails too long,
Dared tell me: "In Amurrica, we bathe!"
I'd have died with shame, had I sailed here to die.
I swallowed pride and rage, and made a vow
The time would come when I could spit both out
In the face of the likes of him. I made a vow
I'd fight my way to power if it killed me,
Not only for myself, but for our kind,
For the men behind me, laughing out of fear,
At their own shame as well as mine, for the women,

HOGAN'S GOAT

[13]

Behind the board partition, frightened dumb
With worry they'd be sent back home to starve
Because they'd dirty feet. I was born again.
It came to me as brutal as the cold
That makes us flinch the day the midwife takes
Our wet heels in her fist, and punches breath
Into our dangling carcasses: Get power!
Without it, there can be no decency,
No virtue and no grace. I have kept my vow.
The mayor's chair is mine but for the running.
Will you have me lose it for your convent scruples?

> [*Pause*]

KATHLEEN

You never told me that about your landing.

STANTON

There's many things I never told you, Kate.
I was afraid you'd hold me cheap.

KATHLEEN

                          Oh, Mattie,
Don't you know me yet?

STANTON

                 Stand by me.
Stand by me, Kate. The next four days count hard.
By Sunday next, I'll have won all or lost.

KATHLEEN

What's Sunday next?

STANTON

The Clambake for Quinn's birthday:
We're to make things up between us and make the announcement
On the steamer voyage to Seagate Sunday evening.
Stand by me, Kate. As sure as God's my judge
The minute I get into City Hall
The first thing I will do is call the priest,
And ask him to make peace with God for us.
Stand by me, Kate.

KATHLEEN

I will though it costs my life.

[STANTON *kisses her*]

STANTON

God stand between us and all harm! There now!
I've wiped those words from your lips. —Oh, where's my mind!
I've brought champagne, and it's as warm as tears.
Go get the glasses.

[KATHLEEN *takes two glasses down from a cupboard.* STANTON *opens the champagne and pours it. They touch glasses*]

Let the past be damned,
The dead bury the dead. The future's ours.

Curtain

✤

♣ 2 ♣

♣

Eleven o'clock the same night. The back room of Stanton's Saloon, The Court Café. To stage left, glass-paned double doors cut the room off from the bar, from which a hum of voices can be heard. To stage right, the Ladies' Entrance. Next to it, a square piano with a pot of dead fern on it. Around the room, squat round tables and bent iron chairs. Stage center, around one of the tables, with whiskeys in front of them, three people. At the head, JOHN "BLACK JACK" HAGGERTY, in his late sixties, wearing his Sunday clothes, his hair parted in the middle and swagged over his eyebrows in dove's wings, his handlebar mustache repeating the design. Both hair and mustache are dyed an improbable black. To Haggerty's left, PETEY BOYLE, a young tough in his twenties, his heavy hair parted in the middle and combed oilily back, the teeth marks of the comb still in it. His rachitic frame is wiry as a weed; and he is dressed in a Salvation Army suit that droops in the seat, balloons at the knees and elbows. Next to Boyle, but facing the audience, BESSIE LEGG, a blond girl in her late twenties or early thirties, her hair in a pompadour under a Floradora hat that looks like an ostrich nest, a long feather boa on, together

with many strands of glass beads, and rings on
every finger but her thumbs, all cheap. Her doll's
face is a bit crumpled, but there is no petulance in
it, merely jocose self-indulgence. There is a crepe-
paper shamrock tacked to the piano, and four
sprung tapes of green and gold crepe paper run
from the corners of the room and belly over the
table in a haphazardly celebrative way.

HAGGERTY

That Walsh from Albany was no man's fool.
The first thing that he asked about was Ag Hogan,
And then about Matt's temper, you know, the time
He nearly broke Tim Costigan in two
For calling him Hogan's Goat. But at last we cleared Matt.

BOYLE

Bess, Black Jack thinks the nomination'll stand!

HAGGERTY

Stop your tormenting, Petey. Of course, it will.
Amn't I Assistant Leader of this Ward
And head of the Matthew Stanton Association?
And isn't Palsy Murphy Boss of Brooklyn
And head of the Edward Quinn Association?
Walsh said that Father Coyne and the both of us
Would constitute a due and legal caucus;
And he's the representative of the Party,
He ought to know.

BESSIE

Yeah? When does Quinn find out?

HAGGERTY

Tomorrow morning. It has to be told him fast.
We're to break the news Matt's nominated Sunday
At the Clambake for Quinn's birthday down in Seagate.

BOYLE

Is both Associations going on this Clambake?

HAGGERTY

Yes. Murphy's got the job of telling Quinn
And getting him to make things up with Matt.

BOYLE

That's a moonlight voyage we'll all be seeing stars.
It'll make the riot on the *Harvest Queen*,
When that Alderman knifed that guy in '87,
Look like a slapping match in St. Mary's schoolyard.
Quinn ain't never giving up to no Stanton
In no four days.

BESSIE

                    Dust off your steel derby,
Or your head will be all lumps like a bag of marbles.

BOYLE

You tell him, kid. I'll hold the baby.

HAGGERTY

                              Lord!
What a pair of lochremauns! That's why Murphy's Boss:

He could talk a Hindu out of a tiger's mouth.
He'll find some cosy way to break the news,
And Quinn will purr like a kitten.

> [*Enter* MARIA HAGGERTY *through the Ladies' Entrance. She is a tall, raw-boned woman in her late sixties, with loose-stranded iron-gray hair pulled back around a center part in a tight bun. She wears a rusty black toque, and a long black woolen coat with a frayed hem, and is carrying a large handbag, which she sets down on the floor as she settles wearily into the chair to stage right of Haggerty, her husband*]

MARIA

                        Ah, there you are!
How are you, Mrs. Legg? How are you, Petey?
I thought you might be waiting here for Matt,
When Josie told me. Why is it so secret?

HAGGERTY

It won't be secret long with Josie Finn
Trumpeting it from here to Fulton Ferry
Like an elephant in heat. Quinn doesn't know yet.
That's why it's so secret.

MARIA

                 What's that you're drinking?

HAGGERTY

Whiskey and water, May.

MARIA

             Give Ma a swallow.

HAGGERTY

Great God in Heaven, drink it all, why don't you!
We're met to celebrate Matt Stanton's luck.
Corner-boy Boyle and Bessie the balloon brain
See trouble in store undreamed by Albany,
And my wife drags in here with a puss on her
Like a lead-horse on a hearse. What's the matter with
  you?

MARIA

I'm sure I'm glad for Matt's sake. He's worked hard,
And he's been good, giving us the flat and all.
But in a way, you know, Ned Quinn is right:
Matt's hard on people, harder than he should be.
He's a lot to answer for before he dies.

BESSIE

You mean Ag Hogan?

MARIA

                    Yes, I do.

BESSIE

                              Poor girl.
When I was there this morning, she looked awful.

MARIA

She'll never live to comb out a gray head.
I've just now come from giving her her tea,
In that coffin of a furnished room in Smith Street.

I looked at the cheesecloth curtains hung on strings;
And I thought of all those velvet-muffled windows,
Those carpets red as blood and deep as snow,
Those tables glistening underneath the lamps
Like rosy gold, in her big house in Seagate.
And I said to myself, if it weren't for Agnes Hogan,
Matt would be a grocery clerk at Nolan's,
And not the owner of The Court Café.
And candidate for mayor; and there she lies,
Flat on her back with two beanbags of buckshot
On her shriveled breasts, to chain her to the mattress,
As if she could move, her eyes in a black stare
At the white paint peeling off that iron bedstead,
Like scabs of a rash; and he never once comes near her,
For fear, I suppose, they'd call him Hogan's Goat,
And his missis might find out about their high jinks.
And yet if Matt were any kind of man,
Wouldn't he go and take her in his arms,
And say, "You hurt me bad three years ago;
But I hurt you as bad. Forgive and forget."
Maybe it's because the girl's my niece,
But I think I'd feel the same if she were not.

HAGGERTY
Be that as may be, what has passed between them
Is their affair. It isn't ours to judge,
Especially after all Matt's done for us—
And you'll set this one thinking how Tom Legg
Left her in the lurch in Baltic Street,
And spraying us all like a drainpipe in a downpour,

HOGAN'S GOAT

If you keep up that way. Sure, what's past is past.
What can't be remedied must be endured.

BESSIE

Say, listen here, Napoleon the Turd,
Legg never found me in no bed with no one,
Like Matt done Ag, if that's what you're implying.

HAGGERTY

How could he, when he worked in the subway nights,
And was so blind he couldn't tie his shoes
Without his nose to the eyelets, his rump in the air,
Like a startled ostrich.

BESSIE

                          Say that again, I dare you!

HAGGERTY

No matter now. It served what it was meant to:
Better glares than tears—

> [*A loud shout from the bar. Applause, cheers and
> singing. Enter* STANTON *from the bar with a crowd
> around him, singing. The four at the table join in*]

EVERYBODY

He'll make a jolly good mayor!
He'll make a jolly good mayor!
He'll make a jolly good mayor!
Which nobody can deny!

HAGGERTY

Speech, Mattie, speech!

STANTON

Thanks all! What will I say!

It's me who should be singing songs to you,
Not you to me. And I don't know how you've learned
That I'm to run for mayor. It's a secret.
Ask the man who told you if it isn't,
Jack Haggerty—

[*Applause*]

When I returned from England

Three years ago with my new wife, I thought
My chances to get back into the Party
Were gone for good. Yet in those three short years
You stuck by me so fast, the Party made me
Leader of the Ward in which the mayor
I had a falling-out with lives; and now
You're bent on giving me his place.
Ned Quinn—

[*Booing and hissing.* PETEY BOYLE *jumps on a table, puts one fist on his hip, throws his head back insolently, and sings, in a nasal imitation of John McCormack. Enter* FATHER COYNE, *unnoticed, through the Ladies' Entrance, wearing his biretta and an old black overcoat shorter than his cassock*]

BOYLE

Is it Ned Quinn you mean? } *repeat*
Says the Shan Van Vocht,
He's in Fogarty's shebeen
Drinking bourbon with some quean, } *repeat*
Says the Shan Van Vocht.

Let him drink it to the dregs, } *repeat*
Says the Shan Van Vocht.
For the goose that lays gold eggs
Lays no more for hollow legs, } *repeat*
Says the Shan Van Vocht.

> [*Applause and laughter.* BOYLE *motions for silence and sings*]

BOYLE
Go and tell that swindler!

> [BOYLE *points to* HAGGERTY]

HAGGERTY
Go and tell that swindler!

> [HAGGERTY *points to* BESSIE]

BESSIE
Go and tell that swindler!

BOYLE
What the Shan Van Vocht has said!

> [BOYLE *apes a choir director*]

EVERYBODY
What the Shan Van Vocht has said!

> [*Laughter and applause.* FATHER COYNE *angrily jostles his way to stage center, the people shamefacedly making way for him*]

FATHER COYNE
For shame! For shame! Have you no charity?
Don't turn upon the man, but on his sin.

HAGGERTY

Father! Sit down. I thought you'd be in bed.

FATHER COYNE

I couldn't sleep. I thought I'd come by here
And have a word with Matt alone.

BOYLE

A word or a drink?

FATHER COYNE

What's that you say, Pete Boyle? Speak up, why don't you,
And show them how malicious you can be,
And you so drunk!

BOYLE

I didn't mean no harm.

FATHER COYNE

You meant no harm! You're all of you alike.
You talk to preen your wit or flex your pride,
Not to lay bare your hearts or tell God's truth.
Words have more force than blows. They can destroy.
Would you punch an old man's face to test your arm?
Answer me, Pete Boyle.

BOYLE

You know I wouldn't.

FATHER COYNE

You did as much to me.

BOYLE

I'm sorry, Father.

FATHER COYNE

I hope you are, my son. Don't look so pious,
The rest of you. You're just as bad as him,
Dancing around the ruin of Quinn's name
Like a pack of savages. Do you know the story
The Rabbis set down centuries ago
Beside the part in Exodus where the Jews
Are shown exulting over the drowned troops
Of Pharaoh on the shores of the Red Sea?
The angels, says the story, joined their voices
With those of the men below. And God cried out:
"What reason is there to hold jubilee?
The men of Egypt are my children too!"
The men of Egypt were God's enemies,
And Edward Quinn's your friend, may God forgive you!

STANTON

That kind of justice is too heavenly
For us on earth. If we condone Ned Quinn,
Don't we condone corruption with him, Father?

FATHER COYNE

You know, don't you, a man can commit theft,
And yet not be a thief by nature, Matt?
Corruption sometimes saps the choicest men;
Sometimes it is disordered sweetness drives
A man to act contrary to what's right.

HOGAN'S GOAT

[27]

Collusion can arise from faithfulness,
And graft from bankrupt generosity.
You know I'd never ask you to condone that.
But once he's made the city restitution,
The loss of office is enough chastisement
For Edward Quinn. You must not banish him.
What purpose would it serve to break a man
Who's slaved for Church and people thirty years?

STANTON

What purpose would it serve? 'Twould end corruption.
Corruption, Father, may be, as you say,
Disordered sweetness sometimes, but in men
Who govern others, can we risk disorder
To save the heart it works its ferment on?
A man may cut away the seething bruise
That festers in good fruit or even flesh.
The heart's corruption poisons surgery.
The pulse of it is rapid. It pollutes
Like ratbite, and like ratbite spawns
Plagues to charge whole graveyards.
Isolate its carriers fast, I say. Disown them,
Before they can infect us with the pox
We came across the ocean to avoid,
Liberty gone blind, the death of honor!—
Would you have the big men of this city say
That they were right in keeping us cheap labor,
Because we are not fit for nobler service,
We dirty what we touch? Say that they will,
And with full right, unless we dare cut free

From these enfeebling politics of pity,
And rule the city right. Ned Quinn must go—

[*Applause*]

HAGGERTY

Hurray for Stanton! The man is right, God bless him.
What answer, Father, can you make to that?

FATHER COYNE

What answer, Black Jack, but the same old answer?
Judge not, Matt Stanton, lest yourself be judged;
Beware, Matt Stanton, lest in pointing out
The mote within your neighbor's watering eye,
You overlook the beam that blinds your own.

STANTON

I meant no disrespect. Forgive me, Father.

FATHER COYNE

Do not delude yourself it is offense
Has made me quote the Scripture to you, man.
I dare not take offense. My task is love.
I have no passion save the one for souls.
Salus suprema lex, remember that,
Salvation is the law that must come first.
My cure includes both you and Edward Quinn.
Because it does, I have to warn you, Matt,
Do not mistake vindictiveness for justice.
I hope you take my meaning. Do you?

STANTON

                                         Yes.

I'll make no move against Ned Quinn, I promise,
Unless he moves against me first.

FATHER COYNE

                                 Good, Matt.

STANTON

For your penance, Petey, draw the priest a beer.

FATHER COYNE

I won't tonight, Matt, thank you. I've a matter
I'd like to talk to you about alone.

STANTON

Sure, Father— Out, the lot of you, to the bar.
The drinks are on the house.

HAGGERTY

Stanton abu, boys.

BOYLE

Let the Jickies and the Prods,
Says the Shan Van Vocht,
Look down on us like gods,
Says the Shan Van Vocht.
We've got Stanton, damn the odds,
Says the Shan Van Vocht.

[Exit EVERYBODY *cheering. Pause]*

FATHER COYNE

It's no good being delicate. If I tried,
I'd put your eye out, Matt, or break your bones.
I'll just come out and say it: go see Ag.

STANTON

Agnes Hogan, Father?

FATHER COYNE

                      Agnes Hogan.
What other Ag would I mean?

STANTON

                            I can't do that.

FATHER COYNE

You can't or you won't?

STANTON

                 One knock at Aggie's door,
And Josie Finn would be scissoring down Fifth Place
With the wind in tatters around her, and at Kate's ear
Before the latch was lifted. It would all come out—

FATHER COYNE

It should have come out long since. Ag's dying, Matt.
Tell Kate about her, and go.

STANTON

                 Whose fault she's **dying?**

Did you ever know her stop when the thirst was on her?
Who poured that whiskey down her fourteen months
Until the lungs were tattered in her breast?
Who landed her in Saranac?

[*Pause*]

                             She was always like that.
Whiskey, or clothes, or diamonds . . . or men!
You can say what you want of Jo Finn and her tongue,
If it wasn't for her, I'd never have found out
I was the goat for fair.

FATHER COYNE

                        Ag was fully clothed.
And so was Quinn.

STANTON

                    You didn't see them, Father.
They were leg in leg when Josie brought me in.
Asleep, I grant you, but his ham of a hand
Was tangled in the fullness of her hair—

FATHER COYNE

You told me that long since. What's done is done.
Don't let the woman die unreconciled.
Tell Kate, and go to see her.

STANTON

                      Yes, but—

FATHER COYNE

                            What?

What can I know of love, a celibate,
Numb as a broomstick in my varnished parlor,
With my frightened curate jumping at each word,
And Ann Mulcahy to do my housekeeping
Without a whimper of complaint. What can I know?
Putting aside the fact that priesthood's marriage
To a Partner Who is always right, I know
If you don't tell Kate, there are others will,
Before the ink is dry on the campaign posters,
And that would be disastrous—

STANTON

Tell her what!

FATHER COYNE
Don't take that tone with me.

STANTON

I lived with her?
Shall I tell my wife I serviced Ag three years?

FATHER COYNE
If you're trying to shock me, Matt, you're being simple.
For forty years, no Saturday's gone by,
I have not sat alone from three to nine
In my confessional, and heard men spill
Far blacker things than that. Man, use your reason!

STANTON
I loved Ag, and kept faith.

HOGAN'S GOAT

FATHER COYNE

                  Who says you didn't?

STANTON

I loved her and kept faith. I did my part.
She played me false with Quinn.

FATHER COYNE

                  If you loved her, Matt,
How is it that you didn't marry her,
Before she, how did you put it, played you false?

       [*Pause*]

STANTON

Not to give you a short answer, Father,
But don't you think that's my affair?

FATHER COYNE

                  No, Matt.

STANTON

It's not the kind of thing you talk to priests of.

FATHER COYNE

You're trying to make me angry, aren't you?
Since *you* won't tell *me* why, let me tell you.
You only wanted Ag for fun and games;
You didn't want her on your neck for life.
You thought she'd spoil your chances, didn't you?
Your chances for the mayor's chair? You thought,

If you married her, they'd call you Hogan's Goat
To the day you died. Your heart rejoiced when you found
The both of them in bed—

STANTON

                  Are you finished, Father?

FATHER COYNE

No, Matt. I'm not. Do you know why you're fuming?
Because you're a good man, and you feel ashamed,
Because I'm saying what you tell yourself:
Whatever wrong was done was on both sides.
The woman made you what you are today;
The woman's dying. Hogan's Goat, or not,
Pocket your pride, and tell your wife about her.
Go talk with Ag, and let her die in peace,
Or else you'll be her goat in the Bible sense,
With all her sins on your head, and the world a desert.
Do you think I like to say such things to you?
I'm trying to help you, Matt.

STANTON

                  I had the right
To show her no one plays Matt Stanton false
More than one time!

FATHER COYNE

              If you'd the right, my son,
Why are you screaming at me?

HOGAN'S GOAT

[35]

STANTON

                              Because you'd have me
Destroy this new life I've been three years building,
Not only for myself but for my kind,
By dragging my poor wife to the room in my heart
Where my dead loves are waked.

                    [*Pause*]

FATHER COYNE

                              Tell Kathleen, Matt.
Maybe it's that which stands between you, son,
And stiffens both your backs against each other.

STANTON

Who dares to say that something stands between us?
That's a pack of lies!

FATHER COYNE

                    Is it? Tell Katie, Matt—

          [BOYLE *bursts through the bar door*]

BOYLE

It's Aggie Hogan, Father.
She's dying; and she won't confess to your curate.
They want you.

FATHER COYNE

          Mattie?

STANTON

               Sacred Heart of Jesus!

          HOGAN'S GOAT
          ──────────────
          [36]

FATHER COYNE

Will you come with me?

STANTON

I will, Father. I will.

[*Exit all three through the Ladies' Entrance*]

Curtain

✤

♣ 3 ♣

❖

Midnight the same night. The all-night Printers' Church in the Newspaper Row of
Brooklyn on lower Fulton Street. STANTON kneels
on a prie-dieu with a framed baize curtain atop it.
FATHER MALONEY sits on the other side of the
prie-dieu, hearing his Confession.

STANTON

Bless me, Father. I have sinned. Three years.
It is three years since I made my last Confession.
I accuse myself of lying many times.

FATHER MALONEY

How many times?

STANTON

God knows!

FATHER MALONEY

With a mind to harm?

STANTON

God knows!

FATHER MALONEY
>Take hold of yourself. What ails you!

STANTON
I did a woman wrong. Tonight she died.
Tomorrow is her wake.

FATHER MALONEY
>What kind of wrong
Is it you did her?

STANTON
>I . . .

FATHER MALONEY
>What kind of wrong?

STANTON
I lived with her three years before I married.
They pulled the sheet over her face an hour ago.
The hem of it gave. It was gray as a buried rag.
She wouldn't have the priest. She lay there sweating,
And they around her with their lighted candles.
She glowered and said, "If such love was a sin,
I'd rather not make peace with God at all."
They pressed her hard. She shook and shook her head.
She kept on shaking it until she died—
Absolve her through me!

FATHER MALONEY
>You know I can't do that.

STANTON

What can you do then!

FATHER MALONEY

Absolve *you* from *your* sin.

STANTON

Her sin is mine. Absolve the both of us.

FATHER MALONEY

Why did you leave this woman?

STANTON

She played me false.
I found her in the one bed with a man—
She stood on the wide porch with her hair down, crying.
I walked away. I heard her screaming at me.
She told me, go, yes go, but not to come back. Never.
She'd rip the clothes she bought me into threads
And throw them in the fire. She'd burn my letters,
And every bit of paper that I'd put my name to.
And she did . . . I'm sure she did. She was wild by nature.
But tonight . . . when I came back . . . she stretched out
   her hands
Like a falling child . . .

FATHER MALONEY

Go on.

STANTON

And I turned away—

I cannot rest with thinking of her face
And that black look of stubborn joy on it.

FATHER MALONEY

Well for you, you can't rest. She died in the Devil's arms
In a glory of joy at the filthy shame to her flesh
You visited on her, and like all the rest,
You come to a strange priest outside your parish
In the mistaken hope he will not judge you,
But give you comfort when you need correction.
What about this other one you took up with
When you threw the dead one over?—

STANTON

Jesus, Father!

FATHER MALONEY

Don't take the name of the Lord in vain to me!

STANTON

I don't know why I came here in the first place.

FATHER MALONEY

You came here for forgiveness—

STANTON

From the likes of you!
For thirty years I've put up with your kind.
Since my First Communion. Saturday Confession!
Spayed mutts of men, born with no spice of pride,

Living off the pennies of the poor,
Huddled in their fat in basement booths,
Calling the true vaulting of the heart
Towards its desire filth and deviation,
Dragging me, and all unlike you down—

FATHER MALONEY

Whatever a noble creature like yourself
May think of me, I'm here to do God's work;
And since that begins with dragging you down to the earth
We all have come from and must all return to,
Drag you down I will. God lifts none but the humble—

STANTON

The pride steams off you like the stink of cancer,
And you sit there and preach humility!

FATHER MALONEY

Take care! I will deny you absolution.

STANTON

What harm! Who can absolve us but ourselves!
I am what I am. What I have done, I'd cause for.
It was seeing what life did to her unmanned me;
It was looking in her eyes as they guttered out
That drove me here like a scared kid from the bogs
Who takes the clouds that bruise the light for demons.
But thanks to the words from the open grave of your mouth
I see that fear for the wind in fog that it is
And it is killed for good. I'm my own man now.

I can say that for the first time in my life.
I'm free of her; and I'm free of you and yours.
Come what come may to me, from this day forward,
I'll not fall to my knees for man or God.

> [STANTON *rises, and quickly strides out.* FATHER
> MALONEY *rises*]

FATHER MALONEY

Will you dare to turn your back on the living God!

Curtain

✤

♣ 4 ♣

―――――――――
♣

Ten o'clock, Friday morning, April 29, 1890. The back room of Fogarty's Saloon. JAMES "PALSY" MURPHY sits at a chair pushed well back from a table, apprehensively holding a sheaf of papers in his hand. He is a florid, rather stout man in his late fifties, with black hair *en brosse*, graying at the temples. MAYOR EDWARD QUINN stands facing MURPHY like a statue of a lawyer in a park. He is a tall, husky, big-boned man in his seventies, bald, but with hair growing out of his ears. He is dressed in rumpled morning clothes.

QUINN

Does Matthew Stanton think he can oust me
By hole-in-corner meetings in school halls,
With craw thumpers and Sunday-pass-the-plates,
Black Jack the plug and the ga-ga Parish Priest
Both nodding yes to everything he says
Like slobbering dummies?— What is it that he said?

MURPHY

Do you want to hear?

QUINN

Would I ask, James, if I didn't?

MURPHY

Listen then. I have . . . full notes on it.
I took down everything that Stanton said.

QUINN

Read it. Read it. Do you want applause?

MURPHY

No, Ned: attention. Here: "My dear old friends,
When Father Coyne asked me to speak to you,
He said it was about Ag Hogan's bills,
A gathering to help raise funds to pay them.
I never thought the purpose of this meeting
Would be political"—

QUINN

"I never thought
The purpose of this meeting"— Father Coyne!
I roofed his sieve of a church and glazed it too;
And put a tight new furnace in its cellar.
There's not a priest you can trust!

MURPHY

Will you listen, Ned!

QUINN

I'm listening. Go on.

MURPHY

"The Party of Reform"—

QUINN

"The Party of Reform"! Ah, yes, reform!
A Lutheran lawyer with a flytrap mouth
And a four-bit practice of litigious Swedes
In a closet rank as rats down by the river!
A lecherous broker with a swivel eye
You wouldn't trust with Grandma in a hack!
A tear-drawers arm in arm with a gaping bollocks!

MURPHY

Will you quit your interrupting!

QUINN

Read on. Read on.

MURPHY

"The Party of Reform has in its hands
Sworn affidavits on the city books"—

QUINN

Got by collusion and by audits forged
As the certificates above their parents' beds!—

MURPHY

"The Party of Reform has in its hands
Sworn affidavits on the city books,
Drawn up from careful audit, and declaring
A hidden deficit of fifteen thousand"—

QUINN

Of fifteen thousand! The unfortunates!
They couldn't even get that business right.
It's twenty thousand, Palsy, if it's a cent!

[*Glum pause*]

I'm in the treasury for twenty thousand.

[*Pause*]

MURPHY

"You say they will expose us to the public,
Unless we guarantee that Edward Quinn
Resigns as candidate in the next election"—

QUINN

See, that's Matt's game. He's out to get my job;
But he's not the guts to grab it like a man.
Will you listen to the cagey way he puts it:
"*You* say *they* will expose *us* to the public!"
As sneaky as a rat in a hotel kitchen.
Don't you see the cunning of it, James? The craft?
It's not my job he wants, but to save the Party!
And all I did for him. I made him, James.
I picked him up when he first came to me,
Twelve years ago, when he was twenty-five
And lost his job for beating up that grocer.
He'd no knees in his pants; his coat was slick
With grease as a butcher's thumb. He was skin and bones.
I was sitting here in Fogarty's back room,
With poor Ag Hogan codding me, when he

Burst in the door, and asked me for my help.
"I'll do anything that's honest, Mr. Quinn,"
Is what he says. He had that crooked grin—
It reminded me of Patrick that's long dead,
Patrick, my poor brother—

MURPHY

Go on, now, Ned!
Leave out the soft-soap. He'd a crooked grin
You knew would serve you well among the women—

QUINN

I should have said, "Go now, and scare the crows,
Raggedy-arse Keho; that's all you're good for!"
But, no, there was that grin; and Ag said, "Take him."
She loved him, the poor slob, from the day she saw him,
Fat good it did her. "You can put him on
With Judge Muldooney," says she; "take him, Ned,
God will bless us for it . . ."

[Pause]

Aggie's dead, James. Dead.

MURPHY

Yes, Ned. She is.

QUINN

Did Stanton get to see her?

[Pause]

Did he?

HOGAN'S GOAT

[49]

MURPHY

> Yes.

QUINN

> She wouldn't let me in.

> [*Pause*]

MURPHY

I'm sorry, Ned.

QUINN

> And Stanton's high-toned wife?
What did she say when she found out about them?

MURPHY

She didn't, Ned. She knows that Ag helped Matt,
But nothing else.

QUINN

> Ah, nothing else? I see.
Where was I, Palsy?

MURPHY

> "All I done for him,"
Fifth book, tenth chapter—

QUINN

> Go to hell, James **Murphy.**
You think it's funny, do you? I'll give you fun.
If it's jail for me, you know, it's jail for you.

No hundred-dollar suits and fancy feeds
With tarts in Rector's drinking cold champagne
From glasses bright as ice with hollow stems,
But tea from yellowed cups and mulligan
Foul as the odds and ends they make it from.

MURPHY

Sure, they'll send us puddings.

QUINN

                                                  Are you mad, or what?
I tell you, I'm in danger. I'm in danger.
Don't shake your head. They're spoiling for the kill.
It's in their blood.

MURPHY

               Whose blood?

QUINN

                               Whose blood but our own.
They turn upon the strong, and pull them down,
And not from virtue, James, but vicious pride.
They want to hold their heads up in this city,
Among the members of the Epworth League,
The Church of Ethical Culture and the Elks,
That's why they're taking sides with Ole Olson,
Or whatever the hell his name is, and that whore
From Wall Street in the clean pince-nez. For thirty years
I've kept their heads above the water, James,
By fair means or by foul. Now they've reached the shore

They'd rather not remember how they got there.
They want to disown me. They're a faithless lot,
And Matthew Stanton is the worst of all—
Read on, why don't you? What's the matter with you?

[*Pause*]

MURPHY

"I would not stand in this school hall before you
If Edward Quinn had not, in his full power,
Made of me what I am. I cannot think,
Since you have shared his generosity
As long as I, that you are asking me
To help you pull him down"—

QUINN

Good Jesus, James!

MURPHY

"The way to cope with the Party of Reform's
To raise the funds to make Quinn's deficit up.
I pledge three thousand dollars, and I ask
Each and every one of you who can
To give as much as possible. Ned Quinn
Must not live out his final days in jail
Because he was too kindly to be wise"—

QUINN

I want no handouts from the likes of him.
Will he pity me?

HOGAN'S GOAT

MURPHY

What's that?

QUINN

You heard me, James.
Will he pity me? Does he think I need his pity!
I made him, and I can unmake him too,
And make another in his place. I'm old,
I'm far too old to live on charity
From a greenhorn that I picked up in a barroom
To run my sweetheart's errands. Don't you see, James?
He took Ag from me first; that's how he started.
He ran her roadhouse for her. "He was handsome!
He'd skin like milk, and eyes like stars in winter!"
And he was young and shrewd! She taught him manners:
What clothes to wear, what cutlery to begin with,
What twaddle he must speak when introduced
To the state bigwigs down from Albany.
He told her that he loved her. She ditched me.
I'm twenty years her senior. Then that day,
That famous Labor Day three years ago,
We'd a drink or two, you know, for old times' sake,
And we passed out, and that bitch Josie Finn
Found out about us, and brought Matt in on us,
Our arms around each other like two children.
And he spat on poor Ag's carpet, called her a whore,
Me a degenerate. Three years ago,
The very year he married this Kathleen,
The Lord knows who, James, from the Christ knows where,
In some cosy hocus-pocus there in London,

To show Ag he could do without her. He never spoke
To Ag at all until he found her done for,
Dying lung by lung. He'd never speak to me at all
If I were not in trouble.
Don't you see the triumph of it, Palsy Murphy!
He takes his vengeance in a show of mercy.
He weeps as he destroys! He's a crocodile—

MURPHY

Ned, I . . .

QUINN

        Ned what?

MURPHY

                I hope you won't be hurt.
We on the Party board agree with Matt.
We feel the time has come for some new blood—

QUINN

"We on the Party board agree with Matt"!
Now it comes out at last! It all comes out!
You and your pack of lies, your trumped-up story,
Pretending to be reading what he said
When you can't read a thing that hasn't pictures.
Did you think me such a boob I wouldn't know
What you and Walsh were up to here last night?
It made the rounds of the Ward by half past nine!

[*Pause*]

Bismarck the diplomat! You goddamned fool,
Pouring that vat of soft-soap over me!
"Because he was too kindly to be wise"!
They'll soon be making you the editor
Of *The Messenger of the Sacred Heart*.

MURPHY

Now, Ned—

QUINN

"Now, Ned." "Now, Ned." Shut up, or I'll drink your
blood.
The only thing rang true in what you said
Was Stanton's offer to be noble to me.

[*Pause*]

MURPHY

I wanted to break it easy. Matt made no offer.
The Party it is will cover you on the books.
But on one condition, Ned: you must resign.

QUINN

I must resign. We'll see who backs out first.
I didn't stay the mayor of this city
For thirty years by taking orders, James.
You tell the Party board I'll rot in prison
Before I'll let Matt Stanton take my place.
You tell the Party board I'll meet the debits

HOGAN'S GOAT

[55]

The Party of Reform found in the books.
You tell the Party board they'd best not cross me.
Don't look as if you think this all is blather.
There's not a one of you I can't get at,
You least of all. Remember that, James Murphy.
How long, do you think, that knowing what I know
About your money, James, and how you got it,
The Jesuit Fathers at St. Francis Xavier's,
With all their bon-ton notions of clean hands,
Would let your boys play soldier in their yard?
Don't glare like that at me. You tell the board
What I have said. I meant it, every word.

MURPHY

The Party will disown you!

QUINN

                              Let them try!
I'll grease the palm of every squarehead deadbeat
From Greenwood Cemetery to the Narrows
Who'll stagger to the polls for three months' rent,
I'll buy the blackface vote off all the fences
Down Fulton Street from Hudson Avenue.
I'll vote from every plot in Holy Cross
With an Irish headstone on it. I'll win this fight—

MURPHY

I'll telegraph to Albany. I warn you!

QUINN

Damn Albany! Get out of here. Get out!

[*Exit* MURPHY *stage left.* QUINN *walks over to the bar door to stage right*]

Hey, Bill.

[*Enter* BILL, *a wiry bowlegged man about seventy who has the look of a drunk*]

Go down to one-o-seventy Luqueer Street,
And get me Josie Finn— On second thought,
Best wait till noon and collar me some schoolboy
To run the errand for me. If they saw you,
They'd know 'twas I that wanted her. And yes!
Send to Fitzsimmons and Rooney for a wreath,
A hundred-dollar wreath, and have them spell
This message out in them gold-paper letters
On a silk-gauze band: "For Agnes Mary Hogan,
Gone but not forgotten." Look alive!

Curtain

✢

♣ 5 ♣

✤

Eight o'clock the same evening. The Haggertys'
kitchen, beneath the Stantons' parlor in the
double set. The kitchen table and chairs are of
cheap oak, varnished and revarnished until they
looked charred and blistered. The chairs are un-
matched, and of the "Queen Anne" style, jerry-
built replicas of a bad idea of eighteenth-century
furniture, with die-embossed designs on the back,
their seats repaired with pressed cardboard. Behind the table stands the big coal cooking stove,
jammed into the chimney. The mantelpiece is covered with newspaper cut into daggers of rough
lace and filled with every kind of souvenir you
could think of, yellowing letters, bills, clippings
stuck behind the grimy ornaments. To stage right
of the stove, an entrance into the three remaining
rooms of the flat, an opening hung with a single
portiere of heavy, warped, faded brown velour on
greasy wooden rings. Through that opening, from
time to time, as the scene progresses, can be heard
the sound of people saying the Rosary. The door
of the flat, giving on the hall and the stairs to the
Stantons' flat, is ajar; and leaned against it glitters
Edward Quinn's appalling flower piece. Seated to
stage left of the table is JOSIE FINN, a tall, rather

handsome woman in her late thirties, with her black hair in a loose bun. Opposite her sits ANN MULCAHY, a small, plump woman with a face like a withered apple, red hair gone white, and fine searching eyes. Between them, its back to the audience, stands an empty chair. They have cups in front of them, and are waiting for the kettle to boil for the tea.

ANN

I'm sure Matt will have luck for burying Ag
And letting Maisie hold the wake downstairs here
In his own house for all that past between them.

> [JOSIE *nods disconsolately. Enter* PETEY BOYLE,
> *swaying slightly, his hat in his hands*]

BOYLE

I'm sorry for your trouble, Mrs. Finn.

JOSIE

My trouble, Petey. Trouble it is for fair.
That's Aggie Hogan that's laid out in there,
My dead aunt's daughter, that I haven't talked to
For, Mother of God, I think it's three long years
September.

BOYLE

       If you come to crow about it,
My ass on you then, kid—

JOSIE

           Sir, you presume!
John Haggerty!

[BOYLE *scurries through the portiere to the sanctuary of the coffin*]

ANN

Now don't be calling Jack. It will cause trouble.
Poor Petey Boyle was always ignorant.
He meant no harm by talking to you dirty,
Josie dear.

JOSIE

It's not his talking dirty
Made me mad. What kind of creature must he take me for,
To come to crow at my own cousin's wake!—
You know, Ag wouldn't see me at the last?

ANN

Nor would she have the priest. She was crazed with pain,
In fever tantrums, don't you know, half dead.
She hardly knew what she was doing.

JOSIE

Ann, you're a saint.

ANN

Now, Josie, praise is poison,
Though I thank you for the kindness that's behind it.

JOSIE

How can you live, remembering what you've done,
Unless you are a saint, or a half brute,
Like Quinn in there!

ANN

By doing what you must;
And begging for the grace to forgive yourself
As well as others when you don't do right.
You just reminded me: I hope Ned's going soon.
It's getting on towards eight; and Matt's expected down.

JOSIE

Oh, Quinn knows that. Sure, Quinn knows everything:
Whose money's stained, and how, and whose is not;
Who's in whose bed, and who is not, and why;
Who has a shame to hide that he can use
To coat his nest with slime against the wind!

ANN

There's a bit of skunk in all of us, you know.
We stink when we're afraid or hurt. Ned's both.

JOSIE

Pray for me, Ann Mulcahy. I've made a vow
On my dead mother's grave to guard my tongue
And keep my temper.

ANN

God in Heaven help you.

JOSIE

It's up to me, not Him.

ANN

Ah, don't say that.
Sure, that's presumption.

JOSIE

Then I won't say that.
But thinking back on things I've said and done,
And my knees all bunions, kneeling out novenas,
If you think that God and all His holy angels
Can shut my mouth once anger oils the hinges,
You're more a fool than ever I took you for
When first I met you—

[*Enter* FATHER COYNE, *dressed in the same rusty black coat and frayed biretta*]

FATHER COYNE

Here in the nick of time!
Who's calling my lost parish's one saint
A fool to her face!

JOSIE

Good evening to you, Father.

FATHER COYNE

Good evening, Mrs. Finn. I'm glad to see
Your three hard years of war with the deceased
Has ended in some show of gallantry.
What was the fight about? Do you recall?

JOSIE

You well know that I do. But what's been has been.
She'd have done the same for me.

FATHER COYNE

I'm sure she would:

HOGAN'S GOAT

For where would be the harm in that, I ask you?
There'd be small danger of much conversation
To thaw your icy hearts—

ANN

Please, Father Coyne—

FATHER COYNE

Dear God, forgive me. I forgot you, Ann.
It's like me to fly out at Mrs. Finn
With the one soul left here I could scandalize
From Dwight Street to the steps of City Hall.
I'll be as gracious as St. Francis Sales
To make it up to you, Ann— Now, Mrs. Finn,
And how have you been ever since?

JOSIE

Since when?

FATHER COYNE

Since Easter Sunday three long years ago,
The last time that I saw you in my church!

JOSIE

There's other churches!

FATHER COYNE

Yes, but not this parish;
And that's where you belong—

HOGAN'S GOAT

[ANN *touches* FATHER COYNE *on the sleeve and looks into his eyes*]

I'm a sinful man.
Pray for me, Ann Mulcahy. I'll begin the beads,
Before I throw my forty years of prayer
Into the pits of Hell to best a slanderer.
Will you come with me?

ANN

In a minute, Father.
The kettle's on the boil.

[*Exit* FATHER COYNE *through the portiere. **Pause***]

JOSIE

I have the name;
As well to have the game!

ANN

He meant no harm.
He's torn apart with trying to talk sense
To poor Ag dying; and he struck at you
Because you brought the days back Ag was well.

[*Pause*]

Will you wet the tea, while I go in and ask
If Ned Quinn can't be hurried just a bit.
I'm destroyed with worrying that Matt will come.

[*Exit* ANN. *Sound of Rosary.* JOSIE *rises, and brews the tea in a large earthenware pot. Enter* QUINN *quietly through the portiere. Sound of Ro-*

sary. JOSIE *looks up from the stove, directly at him, then away. Most of their conversation is carried on with averted faces]*

QUINN

Why have they put that wedding ring on Ag?

[*Pause*]

JOSIE

She asked them to. She said it was her mother's.

[*Pause*]

QUINN

What harm would there be in it, I'd like to know!

JOSIE

You'd like to know? You know damned well what harm.
I told you no this afternoon. I meant it.
Am I your cat's-paw, do you think, Ned Quinn,
To pull your poisoned chestnuts from the fire
And feed them to your foes? I told you. No.

QUINN

You didn't think that way the day you led him
Into the room where her that's dead in there
Lay in my arms as guiltless as a baby
In a fit of drunken warmth she took for love!

JOSIE

More shame to me I didn't think that way!
She was my own blood, and she loved the man;

And I tried to get between them, and broke her heart.
It's all my fault that she lies dead in there,
No one's but mine. And she was good to me,
And I betrayed her— Ned, she wouldn't see me.
She wouldn't let me in the room at the last.
They say she'd not confess her life with Matt;
They say she would not call that life a sin.

[*Pause*]

I'll never interfere that way again.
If it were not for me, they'd have been married,
And there'd have been no sin. Has Ag gone to Hell?
Do you think that, Ned? For that would be my fault.
Have I destroyed her life forever, Ned,
In this world and the next?

[*Pause*]

QUINN

You're talking blather.
Ach, God's more merciful than Father Coyne,
Be sure of that, or we'd have been roasted black,
The whole damned lot of us, long since.

[*Pause*]

Come on.
Wouldn't you like to make it up to Ag, Jo?
Do something for her dead? That's all I'm asking.
Shouldn't Matt pay for what he did to her?
All that you'd need to say's a single sentence,
When the Lady Duchess Kathleen Kakiak

HOGAN'S GOAT

[67]

Descends in visitation: "Mrs. Stanton,
Sure, God will bless you for your charity."
"My charity?" she'll ask. You'll say, "You know,
Ag having lived with Matt three years and all."
That's all you'd have to say.

JOSIE

What am I, Ned,
That you take me for a fool and villain both?
Don't talk to me about your broken heart,
And how you feel you owe poor Ag revenge!
If she had wanted that, would she have died
Without the sacraments to spare Matt pain?
I know you want to drive Matt from the running
And that you'd stop at nothing short of murder
For one more term as lord of City Hall.
Best give it up, Ned. Fast. It will destroy you.

QUINN

Give what up, Jo?

JOSIE

Your pride. Your murderous pride.

QUINN

I don't know what you mean by that at all.
They're out to get me, Jo. I have to fight.
They telephoned today at half past three:
"Albany says resign or they'll destroy you!"
I had to send a letter to that bastard

Throwing in the sponge. But I'm not through yet;
And I'll win out. I always have before.
But if I go down, I won't go down alone.
You may call that pride, if you like. I call it honor.

JOSIE

No, Ned. Not honor, I know. Pride kept me from her.
I'd not admit the wrong was on my side,
And her with the blood of her heart on her shaking chin
In that icebox of a hallroom down in Smith Street,
The wall at her nose. Oh, Sacred Heart of Jesus,
I should have flung myself on the oilcloth floor
And not got up until she gave me pardon.
She'd have laughed at me, and called me a young whale,
Or some such nonsense. She'll never laugh again . . .
What must Matt feel?

QUINN

              Good riddance to bad rubbish
Is what he feels!

JOSIE

          You never knew Matt, Ned,
If you think that.

QUINN

          I knew him well enough!—
You're still in love with him—

JOSIE

                What's that to you!

HOGAN'S GOAT

[69]

QUINN

And him with the worst word in his mouth for you,
As he always has had!

JOSIE

                I don't believe you, Ned.

QUINN

Ah, well. Ah, well. No one believes me now.
Stanton's your god; and that's just as it should be.
You're traitors all, as fickle as the sunlight
On April Fools' Day. But there'll come a time
You'll say Ned Quinn was right.

JOSIE

                        What kind of thing
Is it he says of me?

QUINN

              No matter, now.
You'd not believe me if I told it you.

JOSIE

What does he say?

          [*Pause*]

QUINN

              For one thing that you're two-faced,
And well enough, since the face that you were born with's
Like a madman's arse.

JOSIE

You son of a bitch, Ned Quinn,
That sounds like you, not him.

QUINN

Have it your own way.
I'm old, you know; I'm all dustmice upstairs.
It's hard for me to lay my mind on recollections.
Yet it seems to me I can recall a toast
Matt drank his birthday night at Villepigue's
Two weeks before we had that fight in Seagate . . .
He stood there fingering that green silk tie
That you embroidered those gold shamrocks on—

JOSIE

How do you know that I gave Matt that tie?

QUINN

He told me when he gave the tie to Petey—

JOSIE

You made that up!

[*Pause*]

QUINN

He lifted up his glass,
And laughed, and said: "Confusion to the devil
That's bent Jo Finn as fast around my neck
As a coop around a barrel; and her legs as loose
As her lying tongue—

HOGAN'S GOAT

[71]

JOSIE

God's curse on you for that!

QUINN

God's curse on me? I'm only telling truth.
Come to your senses, woman. He played me false.
And Ag. And her he's married to, Kathleen.
What makes you think you are the bright exception?

JOSIE

Because I know him for a good man, Ned.
And not a poisonous old woman of a thief,
Destroying names to keep himself in office—

QUINN

A thief, am I! I'll get what I want without you;
And when Stanton plays you false, don't whine to me.

[*Enter* KATHLEEN, STANTON, *and* MURPHY. MUR-
PHY *is carrying a case of liquor, which he sets on
the chair nearest him, his eyes fixed on* QUINN *and*
STANTON *confronting each other*]

STANTON

I will not play her false, nor will I you . . .
I got your letter; and I thank you for it.
I'm sorry that my winning means your loss.

[*Pause.* QUINN *glares at* STANTON, *then takes a step
towards the door*]

MURPHY

Wait, Ned!

STANTON

   I swear, I'll see you through this trouble.
I want to be your friend again. Shake hands.
Come on, man. And what better place than here.
I'm sure Ag would have wanted it. Come on—

QUINN

Good God! The goat can talk. When Ag was living,
 though,
You rarely met the livestock in the house!

> [STANTON *hurls himself at* QUINN, *and takes him
> by the throat.* KATHLEEN *screams.* JOSIE *and* MUR-
> PHY *rush to get between them*]

STANTON

I'll kill him!

MURPHY

   Hold him back. Go on, Ned. Go.
Remember Ag, Matt. Please. No disrespect.

> [MURPHY *is holding* STANTON'S *arms.* QUINN, *dis-
> engaging himself from* JOSIE, *blackly looks* STAN-
> TON *up and down, and spits in his face. It takes
> both* MURPHY *and* KATHLEEN *to hold* STANTON
> *back.* QUINN *watches the struggle. Exit* QUINN
> *slowly.* JOSIE *fetches a rag, and hands it to* STAN-
> TON. *He wipes the spittle off his face and coat*]

JOSIE

Pay him no heed, Matt. Sure, what need have you
To care what a thief thinks who's been found out—

HOGAN'S GOAT

[73]

STANTON

I'll thank you to keep out of this, Jo Finn.
You always were a one for interfering.

JOSIE

Why take things out on me? It was he spit at you.

KATHLEEN

Mattie, Mattie, are you crazed or what?
You've hurt the woman's feelings.

STANTON

                          Kate, come ahead.
Where are the Haggertys?

JOSIE

                      Inside with the rest.
Inside in the parlor.

[STANTON *takes* KATHLEEN *by the arm, but she holds back*]

KATHLEEN

                Matt, beg her pardon.

STANTON

For what? For what? Don't waste your sympathy
On that one. And stay clear of her as can be:
She has a wicked tongue. Watch out for her—

KATHLEEN

The woman heard you!—

STANTON

Devil a bit I care!
Will you come into the parlor!

KATHLEEN

Matt, she's crying.

[STANTON *strides over towards* JOSIE, *awkward with remorse*]

STANTON

Josie—

JOSIE

Never mind. I heard you, Matt.

STANTON

The devil
Take you then, for your big ears!

JOSIE

The devil take me, Matt.

KATHLEEN

Please, Mrs. Finn—

JOSIE

Go in now to the wake,
And let me be!

[*Pause.* MURPHY *shakes his head, and motioning* KATHLEEN *towards the portiere, holds it up for*

her. Exit KATHLEEN, STANTON, *and* MURPHY.
JOSIE *walks to the table and picks up the rag
which* STANTON *used to wipe the spittle off himself. In a spasm of rage, she tears it in two and
throws it on the floor. Enter* MARIA HAGGERTY]

MARIA

What's this that Mrs. Stanton's after saying
About a fight between her man and you?

JOSIE

I'm not the kind that would demean myself
By having words with the likes of him, Maria.

MARIA

The likes of him? What is this all about?
I've never heard you talk that way of Matt.

JOSIE

I never found him out until just now.
He treated me like dirt. And who is he
To be so high and mighty—Hogan's Goat,
A fancy boy made good! Ag's fancy boy!

MARIA

You shut your mouth, or I will shut it for you.
Matt's broken up because of Aggie's death;
That's why he lost his temper. That and Quinn,
Bad luck be with the day I let him in here.
I'll not have you make trouble for Matt, Jo.
I want you to come into the parlor now
And take Matt's hand.

JOSIE

It's he should take my hand.

MARIA

Will you come in, if he comes out to you first?

[*Enter* KATHLEEN *softly behind* MARIA]

JOSIE

I'll make no promises.

[*Pause.* KATHLEEN *puts her black-gloved hand on* MARIA's *shoulder.* MARIA *starts, and acknowledges her with nervous heartiness*]

MARIA

Why, Mrs. Stanton!

KATHLEEN

I'd like to talk to Mrs. Finn alone.

[*Pause*]

Maria? Just a moment or two. Alone.

[*Exit* MARIA *reluctantly*]

Mrs. Finn, please. Matthew meant no harm . . .
He has a dreadful temper. You know that.
And he's like a scalded cat since yesterday
When he got the news that Agnes Hogan died.

[*Pause*]

He told me just how much she'd meant to him
When he was starting out on his career.
You know that better, maybe, than myself—

JOSIE

He told you that, did he! Did he tell you how
He lived with her three years in a state of sin
In a love nest of a roadhouse down in Seagate?
And the devil take the talk! Did he tell you, too,
She drank herself consumptive for his sake
Because he threw her over three years since,
When he'd got all he wanted from her, missis,
And married you—

> [KATHLEEN *gasps and runs out the door.* JOSIE *looks straight ahead into the air before her face, brings both hands to her forehead with a slap, and sits swaying in her chair*]

Curtain

✣

♣ 6 ♣

✢

Eleven o'clock the same evening. The Stantons'
flat. Before the curtain rises, the sound of a
scuffle and a cry. KATHLEEN stands, tight with
fury, a large silver hand mirror, which she has
just struck STANTON with, in her hand. STANTON
sits on the edge of the couch, a handkerchief to
his forehead, which is bleeding slightly. KATHLEEN
turns her gaze from STANTON to the floor. With
that sudden recession of energy which follows
drunken violence, she sways and slumps, the hand
with the mirror in it hanging slackly at her side.
She kicks at the fragments of the mirror with the
toe of her shoe, as if she were puzzled by them.
She is very drunk, but on brandy; that is, her
mind is sharper than it would seem to be.

KATHLEEN

The mirror's broken.

STANTON

Yes. That means bad luck.

KATHLEEN

I know it does. But now I can see plain,

Just as it says in First Corinthians:
When I was a child, I saw as a child does,
Saw what I loved as in a mirror darkly,
But now I see his face—

STANTON

                This night of all nights!
When I have Quinn's note resigning in my hand!
The bitch of a Josie Finn with her snake's tongue!—
Where have you been till now? Where did you get it?

KATHLEEN

Did I get what, Matt?

STANTON

                The drink that's crazed you.

KATHLEEN

In your own back room with a woman named Miss Legg.
Miss Bessie Legg. She'd yards and yards of beads on,
And a hat like a berry patch attacked by magpies,
And a fancy neckpiece like twelve Persian cats
All tied together. You'd think she'd blow away
At the first breeze with all those feathers on her.

STANTON

How could you do a thing like that to me?
Get paralyzed for everyone to gawk at,
And with the district whore?

KATHLEEN

                              She's that, is she?
Birds of a feather flock together, Matt,
And whore will meet with whore. That's what I am.
We aren't married. We aren't. You know that.
Isn't it the same as you and Agnes?

STANTON

                              Jesus, Katie!

[*Pause*]

KATHLEEN
Are you hurt bad, Matt?

STANTON

                    It's nice of you to ask.

[KATHLEEN *flies at him*]

KATHLEEN
You son of a bitch, I'll kill you.

              [STANTON *pinions her arms. She drops the mirror.*
              What began as battle ends as embrace]

                         Mattie, Mattie.

STANTON
Oh, Katie, what's the matter with us both!

KATHLEEN
What can a woman say when she learns the man
She left her country and her God to marry

Has married her to show his cast-off mistress
That he can do without her, or even worse,
Only to earn his good name back again?

STANTON

I married you because I love you, Kate.

KATHLEEN

Then why was I the one soul in this city
Who didn't know of you and Agnes? Why?

STANTON

I didn't want to hurt you.

KATHLEEN

                    Well, you have—
How do I know you won't abandon me
If I don't get you what you want from life?

STANTON

Don't say such things.

KATHLEEN

              No wonder they seemed strange,
Your what-d'ya-callem's, your constituents:
They none of them could look me in the face
For fear they might let on. Didn't Bessie Legg
Tell me she thought the only reason Agnes Hogan
Went to bed with Quinn was to prove to herself
That there was someone loved her, when she saw

Your feelings for her dying like wet coal,
And realized she'd lost you? How do I know
The same thing will not happen to myself;
And people won't be saying a year from now,
Kate went the same way as the poor dead whore?

STANTON

Kate. Don't call her that.

KATHLEEN

Why not? Don't they?

STANTON

They don't. And don't you call her out of name.
You never knew her. And the talk you've heard
Has been about her as she was in public,
Stripping the heavy diamonds off her fingers
To keep the party going one more hour.
I knew what lay behind it. It was mine:
Her will to fullness. She contained a man
As the wind does, the first giddy days of spring,
When your coat blows open, and your blood beats hard,
As clear as ice, and warm as a chimney wall.
'Twas she first gave me heart to dare be free.
All threats turned promise when she talked to you.
With her on your arm, you saw your life before you
Like breast-high wheat in the soft dazzle of August.
She had a way of cupping her long hands
Around my bulldog's mug, as if I were
Some fancy fruit she'd bought beyond her means,

HOGAN'S GOAT

[83]

And laughing with delight. She put nothing on
She did not feel, and felt with flesh and soul.
I don't believe she knew what shame might be.
You could not resist her. *I* could not. I tried.
I was twenty-five years old, when first I met her.
I'd never . . .

KATHLEEN
> What?

STANTON
> I was what you'd call a virgin . . .

KATHLEEN
The saints preserve us!

STANTON
> Yes, it's funny now;
It wasn't funny then.

> [*Pause*]

> It was she wooed me.
It seemed—Lord knows, I don't—unnatural.
She was ten years my senior. But, oh, Kate,
To look at her downstairs, you'd never know
What once she was! Her hair was bronze and silver
Like pear trees in full bloom, her eyes were opal,
Her skin was like new milk, and her blue veins
Trembled in the shimmer of her full straight neck
Like threads of violets fallen from her hair

And filliped by the breeze. She bought me presents:
A handmade vest of black brocaded silk,
A blond Malacca cane with a silver head
Cast like an antique statue, the Lord knows what,
There were so many of them. And she'd cock
That angel's head of hers, and tell me:
"You look like such a slob, Matt, I took pity
And bought you something nice. You can pay me back . . .
Some day.

      [*Pause*]

      I took them not to hurt her, Kate;
And when she asked me would I work for her,
Would I run the gaming rooms in Seagate for her,
And keep her out of trouble, I said yes;
And when she asked me would I be her man,
I'd have said yes, but I could scarcely breathe
Between the want and fear of her. I nodded—
I never knew a man say no to her
Until I did myself that Labor Day
I found her in the one bed with Ned Quinn.
I looked her in the eyes, and I said, "No!
I'll play the fancy boy to you no more."

      [*Pause*]

That's what I was, Kathleen, Ag's fancy boy,
I was Hogan's Goat to everyone, Ag's stud.
All my high hopes for power and for office
Fell down around my ears like a spavined roof
When I first heard them call me that— And, Kate,

HOGAN'S GOAT
———————————
[85]

When it comes to feelings, there was my side too:
I might have been some tethered brute in the yard
The way she acted. That last year she seemed bent
On driving home to me she was all I had,
Without her, I was nothing— Even after Newark,
She never changed—

KATHLEEN

What happened in Newark?—

STANTON

Nothing!
I don't know why I brought it up in the first place.
We had a fight. I left her. I went to Newark.
She followed me. We made it up. That's all.
Let's not talk about it. It brings things back.

KATHLEEN

You loved her, didn't you? You love her still.

STANTON

Ag's dead, Kathleen. How can you love a corpse?
And in my heart she's been that these three years—
Part of me lay dead as a horse in the street
In that house in Seagate, till I met you in London.
It was as if God had sent me down an angel
To bring me back from the grave. That's why I asked you
To marry me in that London City Hall
Without the eight weeks' wait to cry the banns,
And come back with me right away. I was afraid,

I was afraid I'd lose you, if I left
And waited here for you till the banns were cried—
I swear to you, on my dead mother's grave,
As soon as the election's past, we'll marry
Right in St. Mary's Church, and damn the gossip!

[*Pause*]

I didn't tell you—

KATHLEEN

Why?—

STANTON

I was ashamed
That I was ever young. I wanted you
To think I knew my way around from birth.

KATHLEEN

Lord help us!

STANTON

And somehow, even more, I was **ashamed**
That I had let her woo me like a girl,
And I could not resist her or say no
For three long years. It was that slavery
I was ashamed of most—

KATHLEEN

That slavery,
My dear, is love—

STANTON

What is it you just said?

KATHLEEN

I'm terrible drunk.

STANTON

Sure, don't I know that!
And if you weren't, Kate, you'd be a widow.
You'd have brained me good and proper with that mirror,
If your eye had not been blurred—

KATHLEEN

But I see plain!

STANTON

Come, Katie, let me help you into bed—

KATHLEEN

You never came to look for me, did you?

STANTON

I did. I couldn't find you.

KATHLEEN

Tell the truth!
You were too proud. You sat up here and waited.
You knew I would come back like a hungry cat,
Like Agnes Hogan! Call to her, why don't you?
She'll stiffen in the coffin at your voice

And drag herself up those dark stairs outside
On her bare feet! They never put shoes on them.
She's back to where she was before in Ireland:
The dirt will clog her toes!

STANTON

Oh, Jesus, Katie!

KATHLEEN

Don't you understand me, Mattie?

STANTON

Come on now, Kate.
The fire's sunk. You'll catch your death of cold,
If you keep up this way. Kate, come on to bed.

KATHLEEN

No, never!

STANTON

Katie, Katie, what's the matter!

KATHLEEN

I looked at her downstairs. I feel afraid.
They say death visits three before it's done.
I looked at her sewn lips, her spotted hand
With the wedding ring you never gave her on it.
They said it was her mother's. Poor Aggie, Matt!
Poor you and me!

[Pause. STANTON *covers his face with his hands and falls to the couch.* KATHLEEN *suddenly throws herself on her knees, and embraces him around the waist]*

I don't want liberty!
Don't leave me, Mattie, please. I feel afraid.

*[*STANTON *uncovers his face, cups the back of her head in his hand, and kisses her temples]*

STANTON

Toc-sha-shin-inish, my darling. Don't be talking—

KATHLEEN

It isn't God I want, it's you—

STANTON

Sh. Sh.

KATHLEEN

I wanted to go away, Matt; but I couldn't.
Those things you said about you and Ag Hogan,
About resenting how you felt for her,
They go for me— Oh, Matt, we're like twin children:
The pride is in our blood— I'd like to kill you,
Or die myself. Do you understand me, Matt!
Don't let me. I am sick with shame. I love you—

*[*STANTON *kisses her on the mouth, lifts her to her feet, and helps her towards the bedroom]*

STANTON

You're crying drunk—

KATHLEEN
                    In vino veritas:
There's truth in drink.

STANTON
                    God! Now she's quoting Latin,
And me so ignorant that all I know
Is that I'm cold and want my wife beside me
Before I can feel warm again or rest.
Ag's dead, Kate, dead.
But, Katie, we're alive.
Come with me out of the cold. Ag's gone for good.

Curtain

✤

♣ 7 ♣

❖

Midnight the same night. The back room of Stanton's Saloon. *Stanton for Mayor* is spelled out in gold-paper letters hanging from the crepe-paper streamers.

BESSIE LEGG sits at a table, looking downcast and bewildered, an empty glass before her, her back to the Ladies' Entrance. The door to the Ladies' Entrance swiftly opens a crack. BILL sticks his head in and withdraws it. The door swiftly closes. BESSIE cranes round, sees nothing, and returns to her glum daydream. Enter QUINN and BILL through the Ladies' Entrance.

BESSIE

Watch what the hell you're doing!
Creeping up on parties like the Blackhand!
Good Christ, it's you! What are you doing here?
You want to start a riot?

QUINN

        Go easy, Bessie,
Or you'll have them in here. I'll tell you what to do.
Go get two doubles; and tell them at the bar

You'd like to be alone in here awhile,
You have a customer.

> [QUINN *puts a ten-dollar bill on the table in front of her*]

BESSIE

> I'm through with that.

QUINN

I'm through with that, says she, and her stairs in splinters
From the armies charging up and down them nights!
Don't sit there that way with your mouth sprung open
Like a busted letter box. Go get the drinks.

> [QUINN *moves out of sight of the bar. Exit* BESSIE, *opening and closing the door as if it were mined*]

QUINN

Keep watch outside now, Bill. Give the door a kick
If you see that bastard coming. If the trunk is there,
And the box is in it, I'll pass you out the key.

> [*Exit* BILL *through the Ladies' Entrance.* QUINN *walks around the room as if examining it before taking it over. Kick at the bar door.* QUINN *starts, looks towards the Ladies' Entrance, then back at the bar door. When he sees that someone is opening the door for* BESSIE, *he draws back into the shadows. Enter* BESSIE *with two double whiskeys in her hand*]

BESSIE

When I say private, I mean private, Percy.

Din't your mother teach you manners— Thanks for nothing!
Pinching a person when a person's helpless!
Shut the door or you'll get a bourbon eyewash.

> [*As the bar door shuts behind her, a* MALE VOICE *chants in falsetto*]

MALE VOICE

Remember St. Peter's,
Remember St. Paul's,
Remember the goil
You kissed in the hall!

BESSIE

Honest, if there ain't more snots than noses,
I'm the Mother Superior at Good Shepherd's!
Here's your lousy drinks.

> [BESSIE *sets the doubles before herself and* QUINN *as she sits down. She pushes the change from the ten across the table.* QUINN *smiles, and pushes it back to her*]

That was a ten-spot.
Them drinks were forty cents.

> [QUINN *smiles again, shakes his head, and motions her to take the money. She does, with a shame-faced smile. They lift their glasses to each other and drink*]

QUINN

How are you since? . . .

BESSIE

You didn't come here for no dish of tea.

QUINN

As a matter of fact, I'd like to ask a favor;
And I missed you at the wake. That's why I came.

BESSIE

You didn't miss me, kid. I didn't go.
Dead people make me nervous. What's this favor?

QUINN

I hear you've been spelling out May Haggerty
Looking after Ag this past year, Bessie.
I wonder did Ag still have a cowhide trunk?

BESSIE

A yellow leather trunk? She did.

QUINN

                              Where is it?

BESSIE

It's around the corner in her room in Smith Street,
The Haggertys didn't have time to cart it home.

QUINN

There's something in it that I'd like to have,
For a keepsake, don't you know. Have you the key?

BESSIE

The key to Ag's room? Yeah.

QUINN

Good. Give it here.

BESSIE

What's in this trunk you want?

QUINN

An onyx brooch.
It was my poor old mother's. I gave it Ag
When I first met her.

BESSIE

She ain't got that now.
I seen that tin box that she kept her things in
Two days ago. That's where May got the ring
They're burying Ag in. That was all there was,
That and some old papers—

QUINN

I'd like to see those too.

BESSIE

Why?

QUINN

Why! To make sure that there are no receipts there
To fall into wrong hands.

HOGAN'S GOAT

[97]

BESSIE

You go ask Maisie.
I got no right to give no key to you.
Those things are hers now.

QUINN

Lord! I can't do that.
She'd go ask Matt; and then I'd never get them!

BESSIE

I thought you wanted that thing that was your mother's.

QUINN

I do. That onyx ring

BESSIE

You said a brooch.
There's something in that box that'll cause trouble.
I'm going to take and give the key to Matt.

QUINN

I wouldn't do that, child, if I were you.
Remember what you told them in the bar,
You wanted to be alone in here awhile,
You had a customer? Shall I call the cop,
What's this his name is, Boylan's on this beat,
And have you up on lewd solicitation?
Would you like a three months' course in sewing mailbags
In the Women's Prison? Bessie, smarten up.
Hand me the key.

[BESSIE *rummages in her bag, then throws the key
and the change from the drinks on the table. She
rises, and walks towards the bar door*]

Where do you think you're going?

BESSIE

Ain't you finished with me yet?

QUINN

Sit down, my dear.
You'll not leave here till the box is in my hands.
You'd be up the street and at Matt's ear in no time
Like a wasp at a pear. Sit down when I tell you to.

[BESSIE *sits down.* QUINN *opens the door to the
Ladies' Entrance. Sound of running feet.* QUINN
*closes the door, returns to the table, and sits down.
He pushes the change from the drinks back to*
BESSIE]

Would you like another drink while we're waiting, Bessie?—

BESSIE

I wouldn't drink with you if I had the jimjams
And every crack in the wall had a rat's snout in it.

QUINN

I know how my morality must offend
A fine upstanding woman like yourself—

[BESSIE *throws her whiskey in* QUINN's *face, looks
terrified, then bursts into tears. With great cool-*

ness, QUINN *pulls a large silk handkerchief out of his pocket, and blots his face and clothing*]

You always were a great one for the crying.

BESSIE

I guess I done some bum things in my life
But this is the first time that I ever ratted.

QUINN

Ratted, my dear? I don't know what you mean.
I told you all I wanted was old receipts.

[*Sound of running.* BILL *runs through the Ladies'
Entrance and hands* QUINN *a tin box.* QUINN *motions* BILL *back out to keep watch. Exit* BILL.
QUINN *puts the box on the floor and kicks it. It
opens. He puts the box on the table*]

I gave that box to Ag myself. The lock
Was always window dressing. For how could I know
When there might be something here I'd like to see.
Will you look at this? A bundle of scorched letters:
Matt Stanton, Esq., Care of the Gen PO,
Newark, New Jersey. That's where Mattie went
When he slipped Ag's tether in Seagate. And look, the necktie
That Josie made for Matt, and a dried camellia,
And a pair of busted garnet rosaries.
And this, dear God in Heaven, look at this,
A letter with no salutation on it
In poor Ag's pothook script. It has no date.

HOGAN'S GOAT

[100]

"You're dead to me, because I'm dead myself.
I have been since you left me. If you think
I mean to cause you trouble for what you've done,
You never knew me. You've made your dirty bed.
Lie in it now till you feel the filth in your bones.
I—" No more. No more! — Ag always was too proud.
She never sent it.

BESSIE
                    Put them things all back.
They don't belong to you.

QUINN
                    Wait now. Wait now.
There's a trick to this false bottom. There it goes.
If it's not the kind of receipt I knew would be here!
It's charred. She meant to burn it. But you can read it.

BESSIE
Give me them things.

QUINN
                    I only want this, Bessie.

[QUINN *puts the paper in his pocket*]

I'm through now. We can part. Don't worry, child.
I'm putting these things in the box, and Bill will return it
And lock the trunk and room behind him. But mark me.
You're not to say a thing of this to Stanton.
He's a worse suspicious nature than your own;

And we've got to come, you know, to a meeting of minds
At the Clambake on my birthday Sunday, Bessie,
Stanton and I. It would only throw him off
If he heard I had been going through Ag's things.
We wouldn't want that, Bessie; would we, child,
Any more than you'd want that stretch in jail.
I hope you take my meaning— I must leave you, Bessie.

> [QUINN *rises with the box under his arm, and
> moves towards the Ladies' Entrance*]

BESSIE

I hope you rot in Hell!

QUINN

                You must love me, child,
That you should want my company forever.

> [*Exit* QUINN. *Sound of a hack rolling off.* BESSIE
> *grabs the money off the table and crumples it up
> in her hands. She looks at the door and at the
> money. She puts the money in her bag and bursts
> out crying*]

Curtain

✣

♣ 8 ♣

♣

Twilight, the evening of Sunday, May 1, 1890.

The stern of a Coney Island steamer bound for Seagate. The lower deck is overhung with an upper, upon which people pass from time to time. There are two oval portraits, one of STANTON, the other of QUINN, suspended from the railings of the upper deck, above entrances to stage right and stage left. Between them, there is a large shield printed in bold Pontiac reading *For the Public Good*. The shield and portraits are hung over swagged bunting. On the lower deck, to stage right, there is a table with a cluster of carpet-seated folding chairs around it. Set off a little from them, its back to the table, there is a carpet-seated armchair.

HAGGERTY, BOYLE, and ANN MULCAHY are seated at the table. HAGGERTY is wearing a green-and-gold sash with *The Matthew Stanton Association* printed on it. Enter MARIA HAGGERTY with a large, loaded tea tray, which she sets on the table. She pours and passes the tea.

MARIA

One hour more, and we'll be into Seagate.
That's what the deckhand says. I'm glad of that.
Two hours more of sailing, I declare to God,
And the babies all would be drunk in their carriages.

HAGGERTY

Where's missis, May? Will I bring her tea to her?

MARIA

No. Let her sleep. She's dozed off in Matt's stateroom.
The brandy must have killed the queasiness.

ANN

Wasn't that a grand speech Ned Quinn made
Before Matt came, on the pier at Fulton Street,
When he said he was glad he'd arranged the Clambake
  late,
So that he could begin his voyage into the evening,
His loyal supporters at his side to the end.

BOYLE

I'm coming. I'm coming.
And my belly's full of gin.
I hear their drunken voices calling
Old Ned Quinn.

HAGGERTY

Don't dance on Quinn's grave, Petey. It's unlucky.
We're not through this night yet.

HOGAN'S GOAT

MARIA

                              True for you there, Jack!
They've yet to make the bad blood up between them.
Father Coyne's been in Quinn's stateroom this past hour,
And Palsy's been at Matt in the Saloon Bar.
Quinn wants Mattie to come to *him;* and Matt
Won't move an inch towards him till Quinn begs his par-
     don
For spitting in his face at Aggie's wake.

    HAGGERTY

Woman, shut up. No call to worry that much.
If you knew politics as well as I do,
You'd see they'll both bow down to a higher law
Before this night is out.

    BOYLE

                        St. Albany,
Pray for us.

    HAGGERTY

              Stop your blaspheming, Petey.
I don't mean Albany, but the public good—

          [*Enter* BESSIE LEGG, *stage right, in a rush*]

    BESSIE

Oh, Petey. Petey. Come to the front of the boat.
You can see the electra light from Coney there,
And that hotel they built like a elephant.
Why don't youse all come. God, its beautiful.

BOYLE

I asked me mother for fifty cents,
To see the elephant jump the fence.
He jumped so high, he touched the sky,
And never come down till the Fourt' of July.

The Fourt' of July when he crashed to earth
He landed near my fat Aunt Gert.
She says you lumpy pig-eyed skunk
Stay off that sauce if you get that drunk.

[*Sound of their laughter fading. Enter* QUINN *and*
BILL, *with* FATHER COYNE *following, stage left*]

FATHER COYNE

You'll meet with him here then?

QUINN

Yes, Father, I will.
I'll meet with him anywhere. But he'll come to me.

FATHER COYNE

I'll go and get him.

[*Exit* FATHER COYNE, *stage left*. QUINN *stands back
and looks at the shield and posters*]

QUINN

Look at that now, Billy.
Brooklyn, how are you! For the public good!

HOGAN'S GOAT

[106]

A whore for a mayor and a spoiled nun for his lady!
We mustn't let that happen, must we now?—
Play lose me, Billy. Here's the lot of them.

> [*Exit* BILL, *stage right. Enter* FATHER COYNE, *followed by* MURPHY *and* STANTON. STANTON *walks forward, keeping his eyes straight ahead.* QUINN *rakes all three of them with his eyes, then averts his gaze from* STANTON]

QUINN

> [*To* MURPHY]

If it isn't the Lord Beaconsfield of Brooklyn
With the ten thumbs of his fine Italian hands
Done up in ice-cream gloves.

> [*He turns suddenly to* STANTON]

                              How are you since?—

STANTON

I'll speak no word until he begs my pardon.
I told you, Father. Has he grown so old and silly
He thinks men can do harm without amends!

FATHER COYNE

Do you want him to get down on his knees to you!
He's lost enough already. Leave him his pride.

MURPHY

The food in the mouth of the voters is at stake,
It's bread and lard for lunch for thousands, thousands,
If this election's lost; and it will be lost
Unless you join your hands and pull together.

QUINN

For all that's passed between us, I'll shake his hand,
If he will mine.

MURPHY

Come on now, Matt. Come on.

QUINN

When he gets as old as I am, he'll understand
It was death I spat at that night at the wake,
And wish he'd come to terms with an old man's rage.

[*Pause.* STANTON *suddenly grabs* QUINN's *hand.*
QUINN *gives him a clumsy bear hug, his face ap-
pearing over* STANTON's *shoulder*]

STANTON

Go on now, Ned. You're not that old. You've years.
There's years of use in you.

QUINN

Matt boy.

MURPHY

They say that when a man shakes hands with his foe,
A suffering soul shoots out of Purgatory
Straight into Heaven, like a lark from a cage.

FATHER COYNE

What Council was it, Palsy, declared that dogma?

QUINN

Sister Mary Asafoetida Doyle,
His fourth-grade teacher.

MURPHY

To the Saloon Bar!
Drinks for all comers, and on the Party too!

> [MURPHY *and* FATHER COYNE *move towards the
> exit, stage left, with* QUINN *and* STANTON *a few
> paces behind them*]

QUINN

You know, Matt, if you left the landing to me,
I could drive it home to all what terms we're on,
And make the kind of an occasion of it
Your missis would remember all her life.
With both the bands of our Associations
Thundering and ringing out below us
And all the voters stamping and applauding,
I'd like to take your wife and you by the hand
And bring you down. A little taste of glory
Has never done a creature any harm—

STANTON

That's just the thing, maybe, might pick her up.
The water made her qualmish and she lay down—
You've never met Kathleen to talk to, have you?
Come down with me now, and I will introduce you.

> [*Exit* FATHER COYNE *and* MURPHY, QUINN *and*
> STANTON, *stage left. Pause. Enter* KATHLEEN

HOGAN'S GOAT

[109]

slowly, stage right. She is dressed in a black trav-
eling suit and is wearing a large black hat. She
stands looking at the wake of the steamer a mo-
ment, moves the armchair into the shadows, and
sits in it, her back to the soft bustle of voices com-
ing towards her. Pause. Enter the HAGGERTYS, ANN
MULCAHY, BOYLE, *and* BESSIE. *They do not notice*
KATHLEEN. MARIA *is carrying yet another large*
pot of tea, and herding HAGGERTY *before her*]

HAGGERTY

You'll have my kidneys burst with all that tea.

MARIA

Never mind. You've a night of drink before you.
Keep moving, bullhead.

HAGGERTY

Have a little respect.

BESSIE

Didn't I tell youse it was beautiful!

ANN

Going back to Seagate's a bit sad
With poor Ag in the ground just yesterday.

BESSIE

Yeah. Ain't it. Yeah. I wish it was Coney instead.
The shoot-the-chutes—

BOYLE

The tunnel of love.

BESSIE

Oh, Petey.

ANN

Will you ever forget the Clambake Aggie gave us
Three years ago, on that lovely stretch of beach!
We'd pails of clams and oysters, steamed and fresh,
And pounds of butter in round wooden tubs,
And crabs and lobsters bigger than our heads,
Chickens and potatoes, roasted corn—

BOYLE

And wagonloads of beer.

HAGGERTY

And good beer too.

ANN

And all day long the men with accordeens
Went weaving in and out us on the sand
Till the stars were thick and near us in the sky.

MARIA

And Aggie, God have mercy on her soul,
Got skittish when they freshened up the fires,
And danced a jig on three kegs roped together,
With all them little bells she used to sew
Into the hems of her dresses ringing thin
Like birds at dawn.

[*Pause*]

HAGGERTY

She nearly broke her arse.

MARIA

John Haggerty!

HAGGERTY

She did! Don't look at me so stark.
One keghead gave, and she went on her ear.
She showed us everything she had that time,
The clocks of her stockings to her knicker buttons,
Acres and acres of somersaulting drawers.
Amn't I right, Pete boy?

BOYLE

You're right as rain.

BESSIE

You was too young to notice.

[BOYLE *pulls the lower eyelid of his left eye down
with his left forefinger*]

BOYLE

Do you see green?—
That was the night Matt found Ag playing tigress
To Tiger Quinn.

MARIA

You shut your mouth, Pete Boyle.

BOYLE

He said she broke her ass!

HAGGERTY

                    That wasn't gossip.
It was a simple statement of pure fact,
To use the lawyer's parlance.

MARIA

                    The lawyers parlance!
Drink your tea, you omadhaun. You're drunk.
Shut up and drink your tea.

HAGGERTY

                    "Ah, man! Proud man!
Dressed in a little brief authority"—

        [MARIA *gives him what she'd call "one look"*]

I'm drinking it fast as I can! My mouth's destroyed!

BESSIE

You should see Pete jigging. He's the best there is.
He learned me how.

BOYLE

                Get up and we'll show them, kid.

HAGGERTY

They'll show us, will they! Stand up to me there, woman,
And show them how we won the branch and bottle
On the pounded clay of every Kerry crossroads.

[MARIA *and* HAGGERTY *begin the jig with* BOYLE *and* BESSIE *doing a little shuffle all their own.* ANN *remains seated, helpless with shamefaced laughter.* KATHLEEN *rises and, standing half in the shadows, watches them with a shy smile. They are too engrossed to notice her*)

BOYLE

He gave it to Maisie;
It near drove her crazy,
The leg of the duck!
The leg of the duck!

[*Enter* STANTON, *searching for* KATHLEEN. *He looks amused; but when he sees* KATHLEEN, *his face blackens*]

I gave it to Bessie;
She says it was messy,
The leg of the duck!
The leg of the duck!

STANTON

What kind of song is that in front of my wife?

HAGGERTY

We didn't see her, Matt.

STANTON

                      Are you blind or what!
You, you narrow-back plug, with your mouth of slime,
You can slather this one all that you've a mind to,
But there are others born with a little shame!—

I'd be amazed at you two, May and Jack,
If I'd not noticed the liberties you've been taking
These past few months. There'll be an end to that.

HAGGERTY

All right. All right. There'll be an end to that . . .
Come, May and Ann, we'd best go inside now.

BOYLE

Wait; we'll come too. I'll lug these things for you.

[*All four move towards the exit to stage right*]

KATHLEEN

Maria, dear, come back in a few minutes.
I need you. Please. I'm not myself at all.

MARIA

Yes, ma'am. Yes, ma'am.

[*Exit* BOYLE *and* BESSIE, HAGGERTY *and* MARIA]

KATHLEEN

Beg their pardon, Mattie.
They didn't see me; and what harm if they did,
They were only dancing.

STANTON

Things have changed now, Kate.
You have to demand respect, or you won't get it.
From this day on, they're to learn their place and keep it.
We're with them, but not of them. —Kate, I've won!
Quinn and I made it up and he wants to meet you.

KATHLEEN

If that's what winning means, God help us both.

STANTON

What's the matter with you?

KATHLEEN

It's being aboard a ship,
It's that, I suppose. When I watch the wake of the boat
Spread out like a pigeon's tail with the wind going through
    it,
I think of all that's left behind or canceled,
And the heart of me feels pillaged in my breast.
The farther away I go from what is past,
The more I stiffen with the sense of danger.
I look around me at all, and want to hold it:
May dancing there with her back straight as a bowstring
Despite the tug of age on all her bones,
And the dazzle of Jack's eyes as they browsed her face,
And Ann Mulcahy helpless with pure joy,
And that dusty weed of a boy and Bessie Legg,
Playing their little games like aging children.
There's not a thing that is not riches, Mattie,
And it all goes from us, darling, like those days
On the boat from England, glazed with salt and sunshine,
We melted first into light like flame and candle,
It all goes from us. Hold me, Mattie, hold me.
Don't thrust me from you as you just did them.

STANTON

Katie, I'd sooner hack the hands from my wrists

Than thrust you from me. As for what's been lost,
God in Heaven be with the days I lay
Like a bee in a lily with the ocean's glitter
Live gold on the stateroom panels. They were good.
But what's ahead, you'll not believe till you see it.
We've won! We've won, Kate! Quinn's arranged our land-
 ing:
You'll be breathing music like the saints in Heaven
As you walk ashore. But let him tell it you.

    [STANTON *kisses her*]

What is that? Brandy, that I smell on you?

  KATHLEEN

I took a glass or two for the seasickness.

  STANTON

Promise me on your dead parents' grave,
You'll drink no more from this time forward, Kate.
There's no sight worse on earth than a drunken woman.
I know it to my shame, from her that's dead.

    [*Pause*]

  KATHLEEN

. . . I promise, Mattie.

    [STANTON *kisses her hand*]

  STANTON

      There now. I'll get the mayor.

[*Exit* STANTON, *stage left.* BESSIE *emerges from the shadows, stage right, and hurries over to* KATHLEEN]

BESSIE

You mind if I sit down? Remember me?

KATHLEEN

Of course, I do, Miss Legg. Please do sit down.
I'm pleased to see you.

BESSIE

                                 It isn't Miss. It's Mrs.

KATHLEEN

Yes. Mrs. Legg. Of course.

BESSIE

                              Was he that mad
Just for that dirty song that Petey sung,
Or was it something that Quinn said to him
That he took out on us? You know what I mean.

KATHLEEN

No, I don't, Miss Legg. I don't know what you mean.

BESSIE

Not Miss. It's Mrs.

KATHLEEN

                          What would the mayor say?
Matt's just gone in to get him. They're friends now.

BESSIE

They're friends now. Yeah. They're friends.

KATHLEEN

What is it,
please?

BESSIE

Oh, he hurted my feelings, see, the way he talked,
And I got nervous. I'm a nervous girl.
That, and you know, what you said up my flat that night,
About there was some mix-up in the marriage.
It sounded so romantic when you said it,
"The man I left my God and country to marry."
I couldn't make it out. You was awful . . . you know.

KATHLEEN

If I said that, I was awful drunk indeed.
You didn't believe me, did you, Mrs. Legg?

BESSIE

Oh, no. Oh, no. But I don't know where you was
Before I went and took you up my flat.
I thought that maybe Quinn got wind of it—

KATHLEEN

I hope you've not repeated what I said.
You haven't, have you?

[BESSIE *rises*]

BESSIE

Excuse me. I'll be going.

Now don't be that way.

                     What do you think I am,
Some kind of rat . . . I thought you was a sport.
You're like the rest . . . Oh, I seen you looking round
When I brought you back up my flat that night.
It's not my fault the place is such a mess.
I only rent it, see? It isn't mine.
And we only just got in when you passed out—
I mean, fell off to sleep . . . I didn't like
To make no noise . . . It's hard to keep things nice.
There was a time I had things beautiful.
When Legg was living with me, Legg, you know,
My husband . . . I passed the flat we used to have
On Baltic Street and Court the other day.
We lived in it two years. I kept it spotless . . .
The windows all were dirty when I passed,
The windows of the flat we used to have,
I mean. All dirty . . . It nearly broke my heart.
I had a lovely home. I used to have . . .
Canary bird. Piano. Everything—
It's not my fault Legg left. Where he is, Christ knows.
Maybe he's dead. I hope to God he is,
May God forgive me, but I hope he is!

         [BESSIE *bursts into tears.* KATHLEEN *rises and com-
         forts her. Enter* BOYLE, *stage right*]

KATHLEEN
Oh, Bessie, Bessie, God in Heaven help us.

BOYLE

Who turned on the hydrants?

BESSIE

Hello, Petey.
Buy me a drink or something, will you, ha?

BOYLE

Sure, kid, sure.

[BOYLE *walks to the exit, stage right.* KATHLEEN
and BESSIE *look at one another*]

KATHLEEN

Goodbye.

BOYLE

You coming, Little Eva?

[*Exit* BOYLE. BESSIE *walks to the exit, then turns
to* KATHLEEN *again*]

BESSIE

Don't worry, missis. Don't. There ain't no call.
There ain't no one can hurt you. You're a lady.

[*Exit* BESSIE. KATHLEEN *walks to the rail and
looks at the wake of the steamer. Sound of a ship's
bell. Enter* MARIA *with a water glass of brandy*]

DECKHAND

Seagate. Seagate. In ten minutes. Seagate.

MARIA

I brought you this.

HOGAN'S GOAT

KATHLEEN

 I won't. I promised Matt—

MARIA

House devil and street saint, sure, he's worse than Quinn!
He's down there now with Quinn playing king of England.
He traipses up to me in the Saloon Bar
And takes my hand and thrusts ten dollars in it.
He's not dead yet! There'll come a time he'll see
There are some things in the world you can't take back.
If I could get a job, we'd move. We would—

> [KATHLEEN *presses her fist to her mouth and sinks into the armchair*]

Good Jesus, Mrs. Stanton, what's the matter!
Promise or no, best have a drop of this.

> [KATHLEEN *downs half the glass of brandy*]

KATHLEEN

Promise or no.

MARIA

 You'll feel the good of that.

> [*Pause. Sound of ship's bell and of the paddle churning water for the turn inshore*]

KATHLEEN

Do you know what I am thinking about, Maria?
How it is this time of year back home in Ireland.
The foxglove has come out in the boreens,
And the seals are barking on the mossy rocks

Below Mount Brandon. On this very day,
They'll dress the loveliest girl in all the village
In a wedding gown, and lead her to the church
To put a crown of roses on the Virgin.
And all the children in Communion clothes,
White suits and dresses, smilax wreaths, pearl prayer
  books,
Will stand around her as she climbs the ladder,
And sing that song that always makes me cry:
Daughter of a mighty Father,
Maiden, patron of the May,
Angel forms around thee gather,
Macula non est in te.
Macula non est in te: Never spot was found in thee.

            [KATHLEEN *breaks into tears*]

    MARIA
Oh, Mrs. Stanton.

    KATHLEEN
               What's the matter with me?
My ears are ringing like a field of weeds,
Noontime in August, when the sun's raw fire.

    MARIA
I wonder is it flashes.

    KATHLEEN
           At my age!

MARIA

More likely kicks. Are you all together, missis.

KATHLEEN

Am I what, Maria?

MARIA

                    Have you missed your term?
Don't bite your lip and blush. You're not a nun.

KATHLEEN

No, I've not missed my term.

> [*Enter* QUINN, *stage left. He stands looking over
> at* MARIA *and* KATHLEEN, *unnoticed by them at
> first*]

MARIA

                    Then it's the dead.

KATHLEEN

The dead?

MARIA

          The dead. Who do you know needs prayers?
They say that's how the dead call on the living,
By whining in their blood.

KATHLEEN

                    Poor Agnes Hogan,
The Lord have mercy on her and preserve her . . .

[KATHLEEN *notices* QUINN]

Don't look so troubled, May. I'm better now.
You know there's a bottle of that Worth perfume
Down in the stateroom in my reticule.
Would you bring it to me, dear, with a handkerchief.

[*Exit* MARIA, *stage right.* QUINN *walks over to* KATHLEEN]

QUINN

Good evening to you, Mrs. Stanton. May I?

KATHLEEN

Please do, your honor.

[QUINN *sits down*]

QUINN

Matt's stuck in the bar,
Buying drinks for all the upright voters,
So I came up alone. It would fill your eye
To see him there. You'd think he trusted them!

KATHLEEN

God forbid he shouldn't trust them, Mayor.

QUINN

If you think, my dear, not trusting people's a sin,
You'd best get out of politics.

KATHLEEN

It's the worst sin.
Without trust, there's no faith or hope or love.

HOGAN'S GOAT

[125]

QUINN

That kind of talk is like a penny cream puff,
All wind and whey, and deadly when it sours.
Trust no one. No one. Let no man too close.
They are as quick to fury as to love.
Once give them purchase, they will pull you down,
And for a sigh let slip, for a ruptured smile.
They're a pack of wicked mutts that go for shadows.
There is no reason in their ugliness,
No justice in their rage. Trust no one, missis.

KATHLEEN

Who are "they"? Is it my husband, Mayor,
Or old John Haggerty or Mister Murphy?
From what you say, you think the people devils
Who've honored you as mayor of this city
For thirty years. Do you really think them that?

QUINN

I do . . . And Stanton is the worst of all!—

KATHLEEN

Do you think I'll sit and listen to your slander!

QUINN

"Do you think this? Do you think this?" Or "Don't you?"
"Faith and hope and love," and I mustn't slander—
You're awful pious for a woman living
With your husband in a state of Mortal Sin;
And a Mortal Sin it is for a Catholic woman

To marry a man outside the Catholic Church.
I don't know much religion, but I know that,
As, I might add, do all our holy voters.

[*Pause*]

KATHLEEN

I suppose you must have got that from Miss Legg.

QUINN

No, my dear. From England. Where you did it.
I've known it years. I hoped I'd not have to use it,
But need is need. And it's not Miss. It's Mrs.

KATHLEEN

You rejoice when people go wrong, don't you, Mayor!

QUINN

We've no time now to talk morality.
We'll wait for Stanton, then go get Father Coyne
And the rest, and walk down to my stateroom
And arrange what we will say. I've bought off those ac-
    countants,
Paid back that little sum from the funds I borrowed,
And the books are doctored. All that now remains is
To find a way to break the joyous news
That I will run again. I think Matt should do it!

KATHLEEN

If you're a man who'd ruin two reputations
To gain your ends, what have you done with your life?

HOGAN'S GOAT

QUINN

What I have done with my life is my affair!
Do you think I'll let that bastard have my office?
I loved the woman that he took from me,
And I let her go with him, but I kept my office.
And I heard them here in Seagate making sport
Of all I'd done for them, but I kept mum,
And I kept my office. And I watched the poor bitch die
While he grew high and mighty, but I kept my office.
Keep my office I will to the day I die,
And God help those who try to take it.

KATHLEEN

Make sense.
The scandal about the funds is a public fact;
But you and Mrs. Legg are the only ones
Who know about the marriage. Spare my husband.
Spare him, Mayor. God will bless you for it.

QUINN

Sure, that's what Aggie said when she pleaded for him,
The first time that she met him, the poor slob,
Did God bless her, missis?

KATHLEEN

They'll never let you run!
They'll gang up with the Party of Reform
And crucify you.

QUINN

We'll see about that, missis.

HOGAN'S GOAT

Do you think I'll let them turn their backs on me
And turn their backs on me for the likes of him,
A narrow-back pimp, who rose to where he is
On the broken heart of the woman that I loved!

KATHLEEN

Pour all the venom you want into my ears!
The Party will stand by us! They'll stand by us.
They'll cover us on the marriage. And they should!
For though we were not married in the Church,
May God forgive us, we are man and wife!

[*Pause*]

QUINN

I wouldn't be too sure of that now, missis.

KATHLEEN

What do you mean by that, you lying devil?

[QUINN *pulls a scorched paper out of his pocket,
and throws it into* KATHLEEN's *lap*]

QUINN

I'm a lying devil, am I! Look at that!
Look at it, why don't you. Are you blind!
How can you be his wife when he married Ag
In the Sacred Heart in Newark in '86!

[*Repeated sound of ship's bell. People are gathering, preparing to get off. Sound of winches, lower-
ing gangplank.* KATHLEEN *sits as if shot, the paper
in her hands*]

DECKHAND

Seagate! Seagate! Everybody off.

KATHLEEN

All gone. All gone.

[KATHLEEN *rises suddenly, the paper in her hand,
swaying with shock, as if drunk. The disembark-
ing passengers look curiously at her*]

God damn the day I met him.
God damn this mouth that spoke him fair, these eyes
That flooded my blood with his face. God damn this flesh
That kindled in his arms, and this heart that told me,
Say yes, say yes, to everything he asked.
It would have been better had I not been born.

[QUINN *grabs the paper out of* KATHLEEN'*s hand
and puts it back into his pocket fast*]

QUINN

For God's sake, missis. Don't take on this way.
We have to keep this quiet. There's people watching.

[QUINN *runs to the table and fetches the half-
finished glass of brandy.* KATHLEEN, *still swaying,
her arms at her side, automatically accepts the
glass from him and, as if by reflex, presses it to her
breast. She does not see the people who are staring
at her. Enter* STANTON *with* MURPHY *and* FATHER
COYNE, *a group of voters around him*]

STANTON

It isn't in the courts reform must work
But in each striving heart . . .

[STANTON *sees the people staring at* KATHLEEN
and QUINN. *He breaks away from those around*

him and hurries over to her. He speaks in a steely whisper]

Look at you. Look at you, for the love of Jesus.
In front of all these people. You're owl-eyed drunk,
With the bands about to fife us off the boat!
I'll get Maria to help you sober up.
Quinn and I will walk ashore together.
You are not fit for decent men to be seen with!

[KATHLEEN *smashes the glass to the floor. She speaks in a ringing voice*]

KATHLEEN

Did you think that—
Did you think that when you lied to me in London,
And I let you marry me in the City Hall,
Because you said you couldn't wait for the banns,
You wanted me so much! Did you think that
When you had me in the bed in sacrilege
Above the corpse of your true-wedded wife,
Ag Hogan!

[*Hostile reaction from the crowd. The sound of the bands suddenly blares out*]

Curtain

✢

♣ 9 ♣

♣

Very late the same night. The double set. There is a dim light in the hall by the Haggertys' door; and the light in Stanton's flat is on full. There are two trunks in the parlor, one already locked, the other open. KATHLEEN moves in and out of the bedroom, packing. Enter FATHER COYNE and MURPHY, the HAGGERTYS, BOYLE, and BESSIE. The HAGGERTYS and BOYLE are laden down with baskets and pillows done up in steamer blankets, and have the tired, apprehensive look of new immigrants. HAGGERTY sets down his basket and unlocks the door.

MARIA

Open it, can't you! He may be right behind us.
And I'll not stand in the one hall with him!—
We'll be out of here before the week is done,
If I have to beg to do it—

FATHER COYNE

Now, Maria—

MARIA

Now Maria, Father? Are we saints!
If he got on his knees to me, I'd not forgive him!

MURPHY

It's grand of you to let us wait here for him.
You must be tired.

[HAGGERTY *opens the door*]

MARIA

I'll not close an eye
Until I'm out from underneath this roof!

HAGGERTY

Come in the parlor, Father. I'll light the fire.
You're famished with the cold. May, bring the whiskey.
Come in now, Pete. Come in all.

[MARIA, FATHER COYNE, MURPHY, BOYLE, *and* BES-
SIE *pass through the* *portiere, followed by* HAG-
GERTY. *Pause.* KATHLEEN *moves in and out of the
parlor, packing. Enter* STANTON. *He runs lightly
up the stairs and into the parlor. He looks at the
trunks and falls into a chair. Enter* KATHLEEN,
*with some clothes. She sees him, averts her gaze,
and puts the clothes into the trunk*]

STANTON

Where do you think you're going!

[KATHLEEN *passes back into the bedroom for more
clothes and returns with them*]

Answer me!

KATHLEEN

I'm going home.

HOGAN'S GOAT

[134]

STANTON

Your home is here with me.

KATHLEEN

You haven't even the grace to beg my pardon!
How can you look me in the face again!

STANTON

It's I should ask that question. It's all over.
They gave the nomination back to Quinn.
He brought me to the pitch of hope and betrayed me.
And you stood by and let him do it to me!

KATHLEEN

It ill becomes you, man, to talk betrayals.
Can you tell me whom you've known you've not be-
    trayed!—
You killed Ag Hogan. But you won't kill me!

STANTON

I had the right to leave her. She played me false—

KATHLEEN

Had you the right to marry me? The right
To cut me off from all that I hold holy?

STANTON

Would "all that you hold holy," our precious Church,
Have granted me a divorce from Agnes Hogan,
An adulteress!—

KATHLEEN

What kind of man are you!
That woman died without the Sacraments
Because in her last fever she was afraid
If she confessed her sins she might betray you.
She died cut off from God to spare you harm.
And you have the worst word in your mouth for her.
Do you know why? Because you're no good, man.
You waited for your chance to throw her over.
You saw that with her you'd be nothing. Nothing.
You had to be the mayor of this city
And she was in the way. You married me
To make yourself respectable again.
That's the only reason.

STANTON

I loved . . . I loved you, Kate.
Kathleen, I've nothing left.
I need you.

KATHLEEN

Yes. To patch your kick-down fences.
But I have my pride too!—

STANTON

Go then, God damn you!
Do you think I'll kneel on the floor and beg your help!
I never begged for help from man or God,
And I won't now. You'll not drive me to my knees!

HOGAN'S GOAT

[136]

KATHLEEN

To sit and tell me you have nothing left!
No more do I! You've taken it out of me
By demanding more than anyone can give.
That's what evil is,
The starvation of a heart with nothing in it
To make the world around it nothing too.
You never begged from man or God! You took!
You've taken all your life without return!
You never gave yourself to a single soul
For all your noble talk. —Even in bed
You stole me blind!—

STANTON

Get out of here! Get out!
You're not a woman. You're a would-be nun!
You were from the beginning.

KATHLEEN

God help you, Matt.

[KATHLEEN *closes and locks the second trunk, and puts on her hat*]

I'll book my passage quickly as I can.
There's nothing in those trunks your money bought me.
Leave May the key. The Express will call for them.
I put the jewelry in the velvet box
In the top drawer of the bureau by the window;
And left the dresses and the sable coat
Hanging in your wardrobe. And that perfume
You bought me's on the vanity.

HOGAN'S GOAT

[137]

[KATHLEEN *walks out the door to the head of the stairs*]

Don't look so black.
You're free now, Matt. That's what you always wanted.
Marry if you like.

[KATHLEEN *almost breaks down*]

I'm not your wife. I never was.

STANTON

You mean to leave me here alone!

KATHLEEN

I'm sorry, man;
But that's the way we all are, but for God.

[STANTON *rushes out the door and grabs* KATHLEEN]

STANTON

You'll not leave me! I'll see to that!

[*Blackout.* KATHLEEN *screams and hits the bottom of the stairs.* MARIA *rushes into the kitchen with a kerosene lamp in her hand, followed by* HAGGERTY, FATHER COYNE, MURPHY, BOYLE, *and* BESSIE. BOYLE *is carrying a glass of whiskey.* HAGGERTY *flings open the door, revealing* KATHLEEN *at the foot of the stairs in a heap, and* STANTON *halfway down the flight in a near faint*]

HAGGERTY

Good Jesus, May! How did it happen, man?
Give me your whiskey, Pete. Poor Mrs. Stanton.

KATHLEEN

Ah, Jack. And May. And is that the Father there?
Amn't I a shame and a disgrace
To get so legless drunk I fall downstairs
Like an unwatched child—

STANTON

                        Oh, Katie. Katie, Katie.
Are you hurt bad.

KATHLEEN

        Sh!

HAGGERTY

                  Petey, go get Boylan on the beat,
And tell him to get a doctor that's still up,
There's been an accident—

KATHLEEN

                    That's right. That's right.
I caught my heel on the baluster and fell.

BOYLE

I seen a man fall off a hoist through a hold
On Pier Sixteen down in the Erie Basin.
His head was bent that way. Her neck is broke—

HAGGERTY

Don't stand there nattering. Go get the doctor.

HOGAN'S GOAT

[*Exit* BOYLE, *running*]

MURPHY

I'd best go too. I've a thing to do, I must.

[STANTON *takes* KATHLEEN *from* HAGGERTY *and cradles her in his arms*]

STANTON

Will you get away from her so I can hold her!

HAGGERTY

Be careful with her—

STANTON

                Katie, you were right.
I've taken without returning all my life.
And I'd the face to call Ned Quinn corrupt!
The harm I've done and called it good! The harm!
I saw that harm in Aggie Hogan's face,
And now I see it in yours. Can you forgive me?

KATHLEEN

Hush now, Matt darling. Toc-sha-shin-inish:
Let others talk. We'll keep our own safe counsel.
There's been shame enough already without more—
Do you know what stopped my breath up on the landing?
I love you still. I thought of us on the boat from England.
There's few have been as happy as we were—
Is that the Father there? I want the Father.

[*Enter* BOYLE *with the policeman,* BOYLAN, *and a* DOCTOR]

FATHER COYNE

Here I am, child. Here I am right beside you.

[FATHER COYNE *leans over* KATHLEEN, *putting on his stole as he does so*]

KATHLEEN

Oh . . . my God . . . I am . . . heartily sorry
For . . . having . . . offended Thee—

[STANTON *pulls* KATHLEEN *away from the priest in a tight embrace*]

STANTON

You're not to die!

KATHLEEN

The boat from England, Mattie . . .

[STANTON *kisses her on the mouth, and hugs her to him, his hand on the back of her head*]

STANTON

Yes, we'll have that again. I'll make it up to you.
I'll make it up. We'll go back home to Ireland.
I'll give The Court Café to Jack to run,
And we'll go home, and take a high-stooped house
In one of them good squares, I mean, those squares . . .

[STANTON *loosens his embrace to look in* KATH-LEEN's *face. Her head falls to the side*]

Why don't you answer me? Don't turn away!—
Where in the name of Jesus Christ's the doctor?

[*The* DOCTOR *kneels and puts his ear to* KATH-LEEN's *chest. He rises with a negative shudder of*

his head to HAGGERTY. FATHER COYNE *motions*
BOYLAN *and the* DOCTOR *out with his head. Exit
both. Pause*]

HAGGERTY

She's dead, you know, Matt boy.

STANTON

You're lying, man!
Do you think I have no feeling in my flesh!
She's warm as a newborn child. We're going home—

[STANTON *loosens his embrace again.* KATHLEEN'S
hair comes down]

I've sprung her hairpins on her— God in heaven,
I was making love to nothing. She is dead.

FATHER COYNE

Get up please, son; let me finish giving her
Conditional absolution—

[STANTON *tightens his embrace on* KATHLEEN
*again and glares at the priest like a cornered ani-
mal*]

STANTON

Absolve *her,* Father!
Absolve your God, why don't you, He did this!
When she found out the marriage was no good,
She packed her trunks upstairs. She meant to leave me.
She never died in drink! She never fell!
I flung her down the stairs to keep her here.

I thought she'd sprain her ankle— Don't come near me.
I'll spit in your face if you come near me, Father—

FATHER COYNE
Go easy, son. Go easy.

HAGGERTY

Get up now, Matt.

FATHER COYNE
Yes, Matt. You have to follow Boylan to the precinct.
When there's a question of murder, it's the law.

> [STANTON *relinquishes* KATHLEEN *to* FATHER
> COYNE, *and rises.* STANTON *turns his back on his
> dead wife and the priest as if in mortal offense*]

STANTON
Maria, lay my wife out on the bed
With some degree of decency, and spill
That bottle of the Worth perfume she loved
Over that bedspread that she was so proud of,
And sit with her until the coroner comes . . .
I will not have her stink, or lie alone—

> [*With great difficulty,* STANTON *brings himself to
> turn and look at his wife and the priest*]

With all her sins on my head, and the world a desert.

> [STANTON *throws his arms out in a begging em-
> brace and falls on his knees. Enter* MURPHY *and*
> QUINN, *unnoticed by* STANTON]

Maisie, Jack. And Petey. Bessie, Father,

Help me, for the love of Jesus, help me.
Dear God in Heaven, help me and forgive me.

[*The* HAGGERTYS *rush to him and grasp his hands.*
HAGGERTY *raises him, and relinquishes him to*
FATHER COYNE]

MURPHY
God have mercy on her. Our election's lost.

[STANTON *wheels around. His eyes meet with*
QUINN'*s*]

QUINN
I never meant to do this to you, Matt.
I didn't know. I never meant to do it.
I only meant to look out for my good.
I'm nobody. I'm no one, if I'm not the mayor.
I'm nothing, Matt. I'm nobody. I'm nothing—

[STANTON *rakes* QUINN'*s face with a blind man's
stare. Exit* STANTON]

FATHER COYNE
Why are you standing round like imbeciles!
Carry her up the stairs, and lay her out
As Mattie asked you to.

[HAGGERTY *and* BOYLE *lift* KATHLEEN, *and start up
the stairs with her.* MARIA *follows, her mouth in
the crook of her elbow, shaking with tears.* QUINN
and MURPHY, BESSIE *and* FATHER COYNE *look on
from below*]

HOGAN'S GOAT

Well you may cry!
Cry for us all while you're at it. Cry for us all!

Curtain

❖

HOGAN'S GOAT

Original Cast

✣

Première, November 11, 1965, American Place Theatre
Directed by Frederick Rolf
Scenery, lighting, and costumes by Kert Lundell

(In order of appearance)

Matthew Stanton, *leader of the Sixth Ward of Brooklyn*—
RALPH WAITE

Kathleen Stanton, *his wife*—FAY DUNAWAY

John "Black Jack" Haggerty, *Assistant Ward Leader*—
ROLAND WOOD

Petey Boyle, *a hanger-on of Stanton's*—CLIFF GORMAN

Bessie Legg, *a back-room girl*—MICHAELE MYERS

Maria Haggerty, *"Black Jack's" wife, the Stantons' janitor*—
GRANIA O'MALLEY

Father Stanislaus Coyne, *Pastor of St. Mary Star of the Sea*—
BARNARD HUGHES

Father Maloney, *Pastor of the All-night Printers' Church*—
JOHN DORMAN

Edward Quinn, *Mayor of Brooklyn*—TOM AHEARNE

James "Palsy" Murphy, *Boss of the city of Brooklyn*—
CONRAD BAIN

Bill, *a hanger-on of Quinn's*—LUKE WYMBS

Ann Mulcahy, *Father Coyne's housekeeper*—AGNES YOUNG

Josephine Finn, *Maria Haggerty's niece*—TRESA HUGHES

Boylan, *a policeman*—TOM CRANE

A doctor—DAVID DAWSON

CONSTITUENTS: Stan Sussman, *piano;* Eileen Fitzpatrick, Jack
Fogarty, John Hoffmeister, Monica MacCormack, Michael Mur-
ray, Bruce Waite, Albert Shipley